101 Wisconsin Unsolved Mysteries

MARV BALOUSEK

Badger Books Inc.
Oregon, Wisconsin

Edited by Kim Sunderlage
Published by Badger Books Inc.

First edition

ISBN 1-878569-70-8

All photos used by permission of the *Wisconsin State Journal/Capital Times* newsroom library except for those of Evelyn Hartley *(La Crosse Tribune)* and Derby Wagner-Richardson (photo provided by Richard Jaeger).

Badger Books Inc.
P.O. Box 192
Oregon, WI 53575
Toll-free phone: (800) 928-2372
Web site: http://www.badgerbooks.com
E-Mail: books@badgerbooks.com

Contents

Introduction..7

1. Who was the skeleton in the chimney?.............................9
2. Who killed Police Chief Elmer Sundby?.........................10
3. What happened to Laurie Depies?...................................12
4. Where is Leo Burt?...14
5. Was Summerwind haunted?..17
6. What happened to Evelyn Hartley?..................................19
7. Who killed Jane Doe?..22
8. Who killed Maryetta Griffin?..24
9. Who killed Jack Van Veghel and Lucille Birdsall?..........26
10. Why did Michelle Manders die?......................................27
11. Who stole the two-headed piglet?...................................29
12. Who killed Officer Gerald Mork?....................................30
13. Who killed Linda Wegner?..33
14. Who stole Hercules Dousman's silver?..........................35
15. Who killed Father Alfred Kunz?......................................36
16. Who killed Sheldon Kliman?...39
17. Who killed Marshal William Gibson?.............................40
18. Why was her ring found on the ice?...............................42
19. Was the Walker House haunted?.....................................44
20. Who stabbed and killed Hazel Williams?.......................45
21. What happened to the Krnaks?.......................................47
22. Who killed Donna Mraz?...49
23. Who killed Albert Buehl?...51
24. Who murdered Kelly Drew and Timothy Hack?.............52
25. Who killed Ophelia Preston?...55
26. Was Edward Kanieski guilty of murder?........................55
27. Who killed Chad Maurer?..59
28. What happened to Robert Christian?..............................61
29. Are there manmade pyramids in Rock Lake?................63
30. Who killed Barbara Blackstone?.....................................64

31. Who killed Officer Antonio Pingitore?............................66
32. Who shot and killed Helen Asmuth?...........................67
33. Who killed Russell Miller?...68
34. Who killed Christine Rothschild?................................71
35. Who killed Tanya Miller?...72
36. Who killed Marvin Collins and Ervin Schilling?...........73
37. Who killed Officer Hans Lindstrom?............................76
38. Who tried to burn down the mayor's house?.............77
39. Who killed Terry Dolowy?...78
40. What happened to Catherine Sjoberg?.......................80
41. Who killed Deputy Walter Gaik?..................................81
42. Who killed Aloyzie Przybilla?......................................82
43. Who killed Debra Bennett?..83
44. Who killed Joyce Ann Mims?.......................................85
45. Who killed Mark Justl?...86
46. Who killed Barbara Nelson?..88
47. Who contributed to Dave Griswold's death?.............90
48. Who killed the Weibel family?.....................................91
49. Is there a Bray Road beast?..92
50. Who killed Milwaukee police officers?.......................93
51. What happened to Woody Kelly?................................94
52. Who killed William Paul?..95
53. Who killed Officer T. Perry Gates?..............................96
54. Who killed Derby Wagner-Richardson?.......................97
55. Where is Mark R. Meyer?...98
56. How did Tim Molnar die?...99
57. Why did Brian Littel die?..100
58. Who killed Florence McCormick?...............................104
59. Who killed Julie Ann Hall?...105
60. Who killed James Elliott?..106
61. Who killed Officer Edward Riphon?............................107
62. Who killed Marilyn McIntyre?......................................108
63. Who killed Michael Fisher?...110

64. Who killed Debra L. Harris?............................113
65. Who killed Dr. Thomas Andrew Speer?.....................114
66. Who killed Connie Reyes?................................115
67. Who killed little Annie Lemberger?.......................116
68. Why did Lorelei Jane Bringe die?........................121
69. Who killed Julie Speerschneider?........................124
70. Why did Susan McFadden die?............................125
71. Was Lawrencia Bembenek guilty of murder?............126
72. What's killing the bald eagles?.........................132
73. Who killed Officer Finlay Beaton?.......................133
74. Why did a Harmony Grove family die?...................134
75. Who killed Dorothy Raczkowski?........................135
76. Who killed Patrolman Grant Dosch.....................136
77. Who killed Dorothy Laws?..............................137
78. Did UFOs visit Belleville?..............................138
79. Who killed Susan LeMahieu?...........................139
80. Who killed Terryl Stanford?............................140
81. Who killed Berit Beck?.................................141
82. How big is Richardson's cave?..........................142
83. Who killed Debra Ann Maniece?........................143
84. Was the Tallman house haunted?........................144
85. Who killed Erik Kraemer?..............................146
86. Who killed Sheila Farrior?.............................147
87. Did the Mexican Mafia kill C.D. Jackson?..............148
88. How many people did Ed Gein kill?.....................149
89. Who killed Lorrie L. Huebner?.........................151
90. What happened to Gregg Kammer?.....................152
91. Who killed Yvonne Reynolds?..........................153
92. What happened to Jeanette Zapata?....................154
93. Who killed Mark Genna?...............................155
94. Who was the woman behind the bookstore?..........156
95. Who killed Wanda Harris?.............................157
96. Why did Vickie Omernick die?.........................157

97. Who killed Virginia Hendrickson?...............................158

98. Who killed Rasheda Dickerson?...............................160

99. Who killed Shirley Stewart?...161

100. Who killed the Balzer family?......................................162

101. Was Jeffrey Dahmer crazy?...163

Index...166

Introduction

When I began researching this project, I wondered whether I would be able to find 101 unsolved cases. I was encouraged by the fact that the cold case unit of the Wisconsin Department of Justice has a list of 90 unsolved crimes, although they refused to share it with a newspaper reporter a couple of years ago. Not only was I able to identify more than enough unsolved cases for the book, but I soon found this project taking a different direction than I originally intended.

I discovered that "unsolved" has various definitions. Police officers sometimes consider a case "solved" if they've arrested a suspect, even if a jury later sets the suspect free. County coroners and medical examiners consider cases "solved" if they've determined the cause of death to be a tragic accident, even if there are lingering questions. And distraught parents may refuse to consider the death of their child "solved" despite what the officials say.

For this book, I've compiled murders, tragic accidents and odd events. I've included haunted houses and UFOs. From the 19th Century murder of Marshal William Gibson to the Bray Road beast near Elkhorn, all of these cases are unsolved or raise questions that are unresolved.

I haven't included all of Wisconsin's unsolved cases and I'm sure there are more that I wasn't able to discover. Many of these cases have faded in the public's memory, although they remain vivid for relatives of the victims. The parents of Chad Maurer still hope to bring the killers of their son to justice as do the sister of Marilyn McIntyre and the mother of Derby Wagner-Richardson. The grandson of

Elmer Sundby still wants to know who killed his grandfather more than 75 years ago.

I want to thank Richard Jaeger, my *Wisconsin State Journal* colleague and friend, who covered many of the cases presented here, and Ron Larson, the newsroom librarian who helped me compile photos for the book.

I appreciate the help provided by Capt. Brian Willison of the Dane County Sheriff's Department, who keeps a complete record of all police officers killed in Wisconsin.

I also thank people who suggested cases for this book, including George Hesselberg of the *Wisconsin State Journal* and our camping neighbors, Norm and Mary. Special thanks also to my wife, Barbara, who provided the support I needed to complete this project and didn't object to me working on it during our camping weekends.

One of my goals in writing this book was to make sure these murders aren't forgotten. The victims of the cases included here certainly didn't deserve their fates, yet their killers have gotten away with society's ultimate crime. I would be very pleased if the information I've presented about a case unmasks a suspect and leads to arrest and conviction.

— **Marv Balousek**
October 2000

1.

Who was the skeleton in the chimney?

Madison, 1989

One of Wisconsin's most baffling mysteries occurred in 1989, when Madison police detectives recovered skeletal remains from the chimney of a business on University Avenue near the University of Wisconsin campus.

The owner of Good 'N Loud Music was doing repair work and had just removed a boiler when he saw water leaking from the flue onto the basement floor. When he shined a light into the chimney, he spotted the remains at the base of the chimney.

"We will be using the crime lab, anthropologists and everybody else we can think of to give us some help," Dane County Coroner Ray Wosepka told the *Wisconsin State Journal.*

Those tests turned up some interesting results, but led authorities no closer to identifying the remains.

Shoes and clothing apparently indicated the victim was a woman. But tests revealed the victim actually was a slender man dressed as a woman. He wore a sleeveless paisley dress with matching belt, button-down oxford shirt, White Stag brand shaggy-pile sweater, socks and low-heeled pointed shoes. He carried an extra pair of socks and wore no underwear.

The case was featured on national television and the face of the victim was reconstructed by Smithsonian experts. Police searched through files of missing persons, they tried to identify the victim through dental records and Madison Detective James Grann stayed on the case for years. But still the victim could not be identified.

Police ruled out the theory that the victim went down the chimney to burglarize the business because the chimney was too narrow. Would-be burglars have been rescued by the firefighters after failed attempts to use the Santa Claus method of breaking into a business.

The business is not far from State Street, the scene of Madison's wild Halloween parties during the 1980s. Was the victim a party reveler who climbed to the roof and somehow fell to his death?

A darker theory is that the victim was picked up by a man who thought he was a woman. When the man discovered the truth, he was so angry that he threw the victim down the chimney, leaving him to die.

The baffling case was the fodder for a true-crime historical novel, *Torsos,* by John Peyton Cooke, who earned a living for awhile typing police reports in Madison.

No one has stepped forward to identify the bones in the chimney and, as the case grows colder, it's unlikely anyone ever will.

2.

Who killed Police Chief Elmer Sundby?

Eau Claire, 1921

Evan Evanson, a clerk with the Wisconsin-Minnesota Light and Power Company, had counted the money collected from weekend streetcar passengers on July 25, 1921, and headed from the Shawtown barn to board a 10:30 p.m. car.

He and a companion carried the money in a white canvas bag. As they were about to board the car, a man wearing a red-handkerchief mask over his face rushed out from a hiding place in the brush. He pointed at .45-caliber automatic pistol at Evanson and demanded that he drop the money bag, which contained $1,037.

The bandit also wore khaki trousers and a dark hat. Although his passengers were in an uproar over the robbery, motorman Claude Ziehlie sped ahead in the street car, stopping at a grocery store to call the police.

Police Chief Elmer Sundby, accompanied by several other officers, arrived at the scene within ten minutes.

The bandit went behind the car barn and walked along the railroad tracks toward the river. Before he reached a river bridge, the robber went into the woods and began making his way along the river bank.

Sundby stationed two young officers, Marshall Running and Lawrence Barney, along the river, then followed the robber into the woods. The officers heard three shots fired. The chief apparently fired once at the robber, who then fired two shots. Sundby was shot in the stomach and suffered a superficial wound in the hip.

The robber ran past the two young officers and into the river. He shouted that he was wounded and would stop and come back. He scrambled up on a sandbar, then continued to cross the river. The officers fired several shots at him, but he kept on moving.

Sundby died the following day at Luther Hospital. A $500 reward was offered, bloodhounds were summoned to pick up the suspect's scent and an airplane was brought in from Minneapolis to survey the area. But the robber who shot and killed Eau Claire's police chief never was captured.

In 1996, Sundby's grandson, also named Elmer, began a

renewed effort to learn the identity of his grandfather's killer. The younger Elmer Sundby said he was cheated out of knowing his grandfather and that the two might have gone hunting or fishing together.

The grandson said people had contacted his father, Russell Sundby, offering to reveal the identity of the killer for a price, but Russell Sundby had refused to pay.

3.
What happened to Laurie Depies?
Menasha, 1992

Laurie Depies, 20, left work at the Fox River Mall on Aug. 19, 1992, and drove into the parking lot of a town of Menasha apartment building where she planned to meet her boyfriend and another friend.

Her car had a bad muffler and from inside the apartment her friends heard her pull into the lot about 10:15 p.m. When she didn't appear at the door in a few minutes, they went out to the lot. They found her car and a plastic cup with melting ice resting on the roof. But Laurie Depies had vanished.

The Depies case was among Wisconsin's most frustrating for investigators because suspects in her disappearance appeared several times over the years only to be ruled out. A $10,000 reward has failed to solve the case.

Police questioned David Spanbauer of Oshkosh, who was convicted in 1994 of murdering two young girls, then determined he probably wasn't responsible for the disappearance of Laurie Depies.

Larry Hall of Wabash, Ind., had a diary that mentioned Depies and may have attended a Civil War re-enactment in Kaukauna about the time that Depies disappeared. Hall was sentenced to life in prison in Illinois for kidnapping a 15-year-old girl. Jessica Roach, whose body was found in an Indiana corn field six weeks after she disappeared in September 1993. Since detectives couldn't determine whether Roach was killed in Illinois or Indiana, Hall was charged with the federal crime of kidnapping. Hall's first conviction was overturned on appeal, but a second jury convicted him again. No charges were brought against Hall in the Depies case.

Police also have received many false confessions over the years. In January 2000, a man was held on a 72-hour mental commitment and questioned about the case after telling authorities he knew the fate of Depies. But the man's story was discounted because of his mental problems.

When a human pelvic bone and vertebrae were found in May 1998 near a Highway 10 wayside at Amherst, police checked to see if they might belong to Depies but found no match.

Steve Malchow, former lead detective in the investigation, said in 1997 that the Depies case was the most baffling of his career.

"I find it hard to believe that there isn't anyone who didn't see or hear anything," he said.

Mary Wegner, Depies' mother, believes that her daughter's friends and acquaintances know more than they've told. Their original stories to police changed later.

"It's probably part of a group of friends that knew Laurie," Wegner said in a 1997 interview published in the *Wisconsin State Journal.* "I think the immaturity of the people involved is why no one has said anything yet."

What happened to Laurie Depies? Maybe some day, someone will come forward to clear up the mystery.

4.

Where is Leo Burt?

Madison, 1970

The whereabouts of Leo Burt, the fugitive ringleader of a gang that bombed the University of Wisconsin-Madison Sterling Hall in 1970, is one of Wisconsin's most intriguing mysteries.

Burt, David Fine and brothers Karleton and Dwight Armstrong were anti-Vietnam War activists at a time when activism had turned deadly. In Chicago, the Weathermen faction was using violence to protest the war. In Madison, the four men parked a Ford Falcon Deluxe station wagon outside the Army Math Research Center at Sterling Hall. The car contained fifty-five gallon drums with a deadly mixture of fuel oil and nitrogen fertilizer.

The four were UW-Madison students. Burt was an accomplished athlete, winning awards in 1967 and 1968 as a member of the university's crew team. He planned a journalism career and wrote for the *Daily Cardinal* campus newspaper.

On Aug. 24, 1970, someone called the police, warning them to clear everyone out of the research center because a bomb was set to go off. Two minutes later, the station wagon exploded in a blast heard up to thirty miles away. Two men were injured and researcher Robert Fassnacht was killed.

The bombers called themselves the New Year's Gang and the Vanguard of the Revolution. On New Year's Eve of 1969, they had taken a Cessna airplane from a private airport and flown over the Badger Army Ammunition Plant near Baraboo, dropping three mayonnaise jars filled with homemade fertilizer and fuel oil. But the jars failed to detonate.

In a statement released after the Sterling Hall blast, the gang demanded the release of three members of the Milwaukee Black Panther Party charged with murder and abolition of the Reserve Officers Training Corps (ROTC) on the UW-Madison campus.

A grand jury was convened to investigate the bombings and indicted the four bombers for first-degree murder. Despite several narrow escapes, the suspects remained at large for several years. Burt and Fine were sighted in Petersborough, Ontario. The Armstrong brothers were stopped in Little Falls, New York for driving a car with a loud muffler and released before police learned they were wanted for the bombing.

Karleton Armstrong was the first to be arrested in February 1972. He had grown a full beard and worked as a gear machine operator in a factory near Toronto. Armstrong fought extradition for over a year but finally was returned to Madison to stand trial. He pleaded guilty to second-degree murder and arson and was sentenced to twenty-three years in prison.

Two years later, Dwight Armstrong, Karleton's younger brother, had made the FBI list of the ten most-wanted fugitives and was arrested in Ocean Beach, California for stealing three pounds of cheese. But the police released him after he served three days of a thirty-day jail sentence.

David Fine was arrested a few weeks later in San Rafael, an exclusive suburb north of San Francisco. He pleaded guilty to third-degree murder, conspiracy and flight to avoid prosecution and was sentenced to seven years in prison.

Police finally caught up with Dwight Armstrong again in April 1977 in a Toronto restaurant. He pleaded no contest to a charge of second-degree murder and also received a seven-year sentence.

After his release from prison, Karleton Armstrong drove a cab in Madison and, for many years, operated a vending cart on the Library Mall, several blocks from Sterling Hall.

Leo Burt in the 1960s

David Fine moved to Oregon and studied law. He graduated from Oregon School of Law and passed the bar exam but his role in the bombing prevented him from practicing law.

Dwight Armstrong returned to the UW-Madison and became a student judge, hearing cases involving violations of student government rules. By 1987, he was on the run again and charged with operating a clandestine drug laboratory near Bloomington, Indiana, where methamphetamine, a potent form of speed, was manufactured.

Dwight Armstrong was captured in Vancouver, British Columbia in July 1987 and sent back to prison.

Fine and the Armstrong brothers have put that deadly era of their lives behind them but, Burt has managed to elude capture ever since the bombing. He was spotted several years afterward in Norman, Oklahoma but nothing has been heard about him since then, despite books and television profiles highlighting the case.

In the mid-1990s, speculation arose that Leo Burt might be the Unabomber, who sent a series of mail bombs to prominent businessmen over seventeen years. Tom Bates, a reporter for the *Portland Oregonian* and author of *Rads,* a book on the case, said the Unabomber's rambling writings revealed that Burt was the culprit.

But Karleton Armstrong disagreed and he was right. Ted Kaczynski was arrested and convicted as the Unabomber.

"I think Leo would come in from the cold if a reasonable deal was cut," Karleton Armstrong said.

"If there was a leader," Dwight Armstrong told the *Berkeley Barb* in 1975, "it had to be Leo Burt. He was the strongest of any of us philosophically."

Burt may have drifted overseas, where Karleton Armstrong planned to go. Perhaps he settled in Cuba or Nicaragua. Now in his fifties, he may be working a respectable job under an assumed name in the United States or Canada, keeping his true identity to himself.

5.
Was Summerwind haunted?

Land O' Lakes, 1970

Wisconsin's most notorious haunted house was a mansion along the shore of West Bay Lake in Vilas County. The house was built in 1916 by Robert P. Lamont, who became U.S. commerce secretary in 1929 under President Herbert Hoover.

In the early 1970s, Arnold and Ginger Hinshaw noticed strange things about the house almost from the day they moved in. They heard voices and noticed vague shapes moving down the mansion's hallways. While they ate dinner each night, the family watched the ghost of a woman float back and forth.

Windows and doors were closed at night, but found open in the morning. Appliances, such as a new water heater, broke down, and miraculously fixed themselves.

When the Hinshaws tried to hired workers to restore the house, they often failed to show up because they didn't want to work on the haunted house.

While painting a closet one day, the couple removed a large show drawer along the back wall and discovered a hidden space behind it. When Arnold Hinshaw shined a flashlight into the opening, he saw a corpse jammed inside. The Hinshaw's two children also saw parts of the body when they crawled into the opening. Later, however, the corpse mysteriously disappeared.

When Arnold went outside to start his car one day to go to work, the car burst into flames for no apparent reason.

Arnold began staying up late at night playing the family's Hammond organ. His playing took on a Hitchcockian frenzy, keeping the family awake with noise that barely resembled music. After Arnold attempted suicide, he began psychiatric treatment for a breakdown.

Ginger Hinshaw and the children went to live with her parents in Granton. She divorced Arnold and married George Olsen. Then Ginger's father, Raymond Bober, said he was going to buy the house now called Summerwind so he and his wife, Marie, could open a restaurant.

Bober said he knew the mansion was haunted and that he knew the ghost was Jonathan Carver, the English explorer who was searching for an old deed given him by the Sioux tribe that supposedly was hidden in the house's foundation. The vision of Carver's ghost had come to Bober in a dream. The problem was that there was no historical evidence Carver ever traveled that far north and the Sioux never owned land east of the Mississippi River..

But Bober wrote about his Carver ghost theory in *The Carver Effect,* a book he published under the pseudonym of Wolfgang von Bober in 1979.

On one occasion, when Karl Bober, Ginger's brother, went alone to Summerwind, he heard the sound of two gunshots coming from the kitchen and smelled gunpowder. But no one else was around who could have fired a gun. He found two old bullet holes in a door leading to the basement.

Bober claimed in his book that Robert Lamont, who had built the house, once fired two shots at a ghost.

Bober never renovated the house for his restaurant and he never could determine accurate room dimensions, which seemed to shrink or expand from day to day.

During the 1980s, Summerwind became a tourist attraction to the dismay of local residents who never believed the place was haunted. The house burned down in the 1990s and only the chimney remained. Some people said those who stole chimney bricks were punished with bad luck.

6.

What happened to Evelyn Hartley?

La Crosse, 1953

Evelyn Hartley was one of those brainy, bespectacled girls with few boyfriends. She was a shy, high school junior with a straight-A average. Her family had moved to La Crosse four years earlier from Charleston, Illinois.

On the night of October 24, 1953, Evie was picked up by Viggio Rasmusen, a physics professor, and taken to the Rasmusen home to baby-sit for his twenty-month-old daughter, Janis. The Rasmusens were going to the La Crosse State homecoming football game against River Falls. It was Evie's first baby-sitting job in three months.

Neighbors later reported they heard screams about 7:15 p.m. but dismissed them as coming from children at play. By 9:30 p.m., however, Evie's parents grew worried because she hadn't called them as she always did when she was baby-sitting.

Evie's father drove to the Rasmusen house, where he found the doors locked, the lights on and the radio playing. He rang both the front and back doorbells, then pounded on the doors and shouted for Evie, but got no response.

He walked around the house and found a basement window had been opened, possibly by an intruder. When he crawled inside, Hartley found Janis sleeping peacefully in a basement crib. He found one of Evie's shoes at the bottom of the stairs but still no sign of his daughter.

Hartley called the police. When officers arrived, they found pry marks on a bedroom window and blood stains on the ground outside the home. More blood was found smeared on a neighbor's house and across a nearby garage.

Tracking dogs were brought to the scene. Four times they picked up a trail, but stopped each time about two blocks from the house, where officers surmised Evie had been forced into a car.

Evie's disappearance stirred the outrage of thousands

in the Mississippi River city. Local radio stations put out pleas for volunteers. More than a thousand people showed up and organized groups of thirty to sixty searchers who checked under manhole covers down every city street in La Crosse. Boy Scouts and members of the Civil Air Patrol joined Evie's Central High School classmates in a massive sweep of a wooded, marshy area at the southeastern edge of the city.

The disappearance terrified the city. A curfew was imposed banning teenagers from the streets after 10 p.m. Husbands stayed home from work so they wouldn't leave their wives home alone. The demand for baby-sitters reached an all-time low.

Evelyn Hartley

Three days after Evie vanished, a blood-stained brassiere and panties were found under a Highway 14 overpass about two miles south of the Rasmusen home. The undergarments were Evie's size.

Farther east on Highway 14, police found a black pair of bloody tennis shoes that matched footprints found in a flower bed outside the Rasmusen home. A ragged blue denim jacket was discovered nearby. A pair of trousers found in the same area had Type A blood stains, which matched Evie's blood type.

An examination of the jacket revealed a faded spot under the armpits that led investigators to believe that the owner was a steeple jack who had worn a harness to work on towers and smokestacks. The blood stains on the jacket were not from an injury to the person wearing it. Thread counts of the jacket and fibers found at the Rasmusen home indicated the jacket was worn by Evie's abductor.

Detectives found a La Crosse businessman who made harnesses for two steeplejacks during the summer of 1952, the year before Evie vanished. He recalled that the customers were young and probably from the area.

Like the faded spots on the denim jacket, however, the leads themselves soon faded away. A private investigator was hired, but no suspect was identified.

In 1985, La Crosse Police Chief William Reynolds said many people believed notorious Plainfield killer Ed Gein was responsible for Evie's abduction and murder. In a book about Gein by Judge Robert H. Gollmar, the judge wrote that sexual organs of two young girls were found at Gein's farm although no young girls were buried at nearby cemeteries during the killer's grave-robbing forays. Gollmar, who tried the Gein case, also said that Gein apparently was in La Crosse on the weekend Evie disappeared to visit an aunt who lived two blocks from the Rasmusen home.

Others speculate that Evie's body was buried under concrete during highway construction that summer.

Did Ed Gein whisk Evie to her death? Or was it someone else?

7.
Who killed Jane Doe?
Westby, 1984

In Vernon County, she's known as Jane Doe. She was buried in a shallow grave in the Viroqua Cemetery beneath a marker that read: "Jane Doe, found May 4, 1984."

She was probably in her late sixties when she was

beaten to death and dumped in a roadside ditch about five miles west of Westby. Her hands were severed at the wrist, probably to hide her identity and avoid the possibility of fingerprints. They were never found.

The woman's body was discovered by three teen-agers along a gravel road in Strangstalien Valley, not far from Highway 14.

During the 1980s, Vernon County authorities distributed thousands of posters nationwide with a composite drawing of the woman and a description of how she was found. Her story was told in magazines, crime bulletins and a national nursing home publication. Identification numbers found on the upper plate of her dentures were published in a national dental journal.

Details about the case were sent to women's prisons as well as sheriff's and police departments. Her death was discussed at police conferences and in news stories.

Still, detectives have not been able to identify her. Police believe if they learn the woman's identity, they will find the killer. Otherwise, the killer wouldn't have gone to the trouble of hiding the woman's identity.

"You know, there are a lot of angles, a lot of things to think of in a case like this," said former Vernon County Undersheriff Jerry Fredrickson, who headed the investigation during the 1980s. "People say, 'How can someone drop out of society and not be missed?' Well, there are ways."

Lila Morrison, the wife of cemetery caretaker Clair Morrison, spotted one suspicious person that visited the woman's grave the fall after she was buried.

Morrison said it was a small, slender person dressed as a woman but whom she believed walked like a man. The visitor wore a red wig and an out-of-style bell-bottomed pant suit.

"He just stood there, looking at the grave," Morrison told a *Wisconsin State Journal* reporter. "He walked around a bit and then jumped into the car and left."

Was the strange graveyard visitor somehow connected to the woman's death? Who was the woman who died so brutally? The case has grown cold and may never be solved.

8.

Who killed Maryetta Griffin?

Milwaukee, 1998

Maryetta Griffin had cancer when she died but the disease didn't kill her. Her death was a violent end to a harsh life.

Griffin, 39, was found strangled to death on February 17, 1998, in a garage on Milwaukee's North Side. A blue high school letter sweater was pulled over her head and she also was wearing a bra and green shirt. She was naked from the waist down. She had abrasions on her jaw, chin and fingers.

The garage where Griffin was found was near a vacant upstairs apartment that police believed was a center for crack dealing. Blood was found on the steps leading from the house to the garage, and police said someone bleeding may have been carried down the steps. Witnesses said they saw Griffin going into the upstairs apartment the day before her body was found.

She was a crack addict, had 28 prostitution arrests on her criminal record and was one of a dozen women, mostly prostitutes, killed in the same area during the decade. She had refused treatment for cancer.

Shortly before her death, Griffin told a friend she thought that maybe it was time for her to die. She was one of a dozen black women killed in Milwaukee over a 10-year period.

When she was 13, her father was shot six times and killed in a tavern. At age 26, Griffin's throat and faced were slashed, she was raped and left for dead in a field. The father of her children died when his motorcycle was rear-ended by a drunken driver.

Griffin's murder was similar to several others linked to George L. "Mule" Jones. These women were strangled with the killer's bare hands while others were strangled with rope. But Jones couldn't be blamed for this murder because he was in jail at the time.

Griffin's body was found a block from where Florence McCormick was found strangled with a clothesline in 1995.

Court records showed Griffin once offered to perform a sex act for $30 and a pack of Newport cigarettes. Her uncle, Joseph Cocroft, told police she lived a fast life with a history of heavy drinking, prostitution and crack cocaine. She had been arrested 51 times and twice propositioned the same undercover officer.

William Avery was arrested for Griffin's murder. He admitted he had been with Griffin early that day and that he had grabbed her. But he said he forgot everything else about the encounter.

Police were unable to make the murder charge stick against Avery, although he was sentenced to ten years in prison later that year for running a drug house. Did Avery kill Maryetta Griffin or did someone else get away with murder?

9.

Who killed Jack Van Veghel and Lucille Birdsall?

Green Bay, 1930

Jack Van Veghel operated a restaurant in Green Bay during the Roaring Twenties. Lucille Birdsall was a waitress who worked for him.

In May 1930, Van Veghel and Birdsall were found hacked to death with a hatchet inside the restaurant. They apparently were killed after closing for the night. No weapon was found and no one ever was charged with the crime.

The case baffled detectives for decades and not even a seance more than forty years later could unearth details about the killer.

In 1974, the restaurant was called the Don Quixote Supper Club when Peter and Philip Lee bought it from Eddie Weber. The Lee brothers, from China, converted it into a Cantonese restaurant.

Shortly after buying the restaurant, Peter Lee was staying in the empty apartment upstairs.

"I heard someone trying to talk on the telephone," he said. "For a half hour a woman was trying to talk on the phone. I was really scared."

When he checked on the sound, he found the telephone line was disconnected.

"The phone was completely dead, but I heard it for two nights," he said.

The telephone incident wasn't the only weird happening at the bar. Glasses also shattered for no reason. A bartender would put a glass on the bar and it would shatter without anyone touching it.

The odd events always seemed to occur in May, near the anniversary of the brutal murder.

The Lee brothers recruited professional psychic David Ray of Neenah to unravel the mystery with a seance in May 1990. Diners participated in the seance, submitting written questions to Ray. The seance concluded that spirits inhabited the building, but shed no light on the murders.

The brothers and restaurant employees held another seance with a Ouija board but still couldn't solve the murders.

Do spirits inhabit the popular Cantonese restaurant? Are they the ghosts of Jack Van Veghel and Lucille Birdsall? Who killed the restaurant operator and waitress?

10.
Why did Michelle Manders die?
Watertown, 1981

Little Michelle Manders, age 2, liked to wander the neighborhood with her pet dog. Once she learned to walk, there was no stopping her.

One day, she was found in an alley behind Trinity St. Luke's Lutheran School and had to be taken to her home a block away by a teacher. Michelle didn't know where she lived, but her puppy often found their way home.

On October 13, 1981, however, Michelle took her last walk. When the pretty blonde toddler vanished from her home, her disappearance raised the specter of foul play.

The case took a different turn when a family friend told

police she gave little Michelle her mother's purse and let the toddler out of the house after 10:30 p.m. the night before she was discovered missing. The woman told police she last saw Michelle standing in the driveway in her pajamas. The purse with its contents scattered was found a block from the Manders home. The woman was not arrested.

"There is no indication of any act of criminal involvement on her part," Watertown Police Chief Richard Reynolds told a *Wisconsin State Journal* reporter.

Michelle's parents feared she had been kidnapped and a massive search was launched for the missing girl. Students at the Trinity school helped authorities look for her.

On Nov. 5, nearly a month after her disappearance, Michelle's body was found in the icy Rock River. An autopsy determined that drowning was the cause of her death. But investigators still weren't sure how or why Michelle left the house that night and why she died. Was she abducted or did she just wander away that night?

Michelle's parents hired Milwaukee private investigator Norbert Kurczewski, who said he found some evidence that Michelle was seen in the company of a middle-aged couple shortly after her disappearance. Kurczewski said some people saw the man and women with Michelle in a restaurant in Black Earth. He said Michelle appeared "fussy," and looked like she didn't belong with the two adults.

Later, Kurczewski would make an even more startling claim: That a cult was responsible for Michelle's death as well as other unsolved area murders.

The private investigator said the former wife of a convicted child molester found maps showing a small red devil drawn in the margin. He claimed the devil's tail pointed to the location of Michelle's body along with those of Tim Hack and Kelly Drew. He said the drawing also tied the child molester to the 1978 disappearance of Catherine Sjoberg.

Kurczewski claimed the child molester, a defrocked priest and several former nuns practiced "black masses." The child molester had books on witchcraft, satanic ceremonies and human sacrifice.

Michelle's death had been ruled an accidental drowning and authorities discounted Kurczewski's claims.

"We saw the picture and the maps and we talked to the ex-wife," Harry Buerger, chief deputy of the Jefferson County Sheriff's Department told a *Wisconsin State Journal* reporter in 1983. "We didn't see any devils on the maps we were shown. They were plat maps with penciled in circles on them which could have been the location of jobs the woman's ex-husband had. He was a painter and worked throughout the county."

Was Michelle abducted that night by a satanic cult? Or did she just wander away and fall into the Rock River?

11.

Who stole the two-headed piglet?

Poynette, 1999

MacKenzie Environmental Education Center near Poynette in southern Columbia County is a popular destination for spring class field trips.

The center features a variety of animals for children to observe and a few other oddities like the two-headed piglet, an attraction at the center for four decades. For many years, the piglet was displayed with a four-legged pheasant chick and a pair of raccoons joined at the back.

On May 20, 1999, someone broke into the center and stole the two-headed piglet, which was preserved in a jar. The thief also did several hundred dollars worth of damage to the center.

News of the theft resulted in a flood of calls to the center from those who had visited over the years. A farmer offered a two-bodied, one-headed piglet he had preserved in a jar as a replacement for the missing piglet.

As publicity about the theft mounted, the pressure on the thief apparently grew too heavy of a burden. Someone squealed, calling a Crime Stoppers line to say that the missing piglet could be found along a walking path near the center.

The piglet was taken to Divine Savior Hospital in Portage for a fresh jar of formaldehyde and put back on display at the center. The pignapper, however, remains at large.

12.

Who killed Officer Gerald Mork?

Iola, 1985

When Iola Police Officer Gerald Mork was found shot to death in his squad car July 14, 1985, suspicion turned on some motorcyclists Mork had confronted earlier in the evening for failure to pay their bill at a local restaurant.

The motorcyclists had eventually paid their tab and left. But had they later confronted Mork and killed him?

The 31-year-old officer was shot twice at close range and Coroner Lloyd Maasch said one of the bullets pierced his skull. Mork was working overtime that weekend because Iola was the site of the annual Old Car Show, which drew 80,000 people.

Mork, one of two full-time Iola officers and the son of Waupaca County Sheriff William Mork, was found lying face down near his squad car parked in Riverside Cemetery after he failed to respond to police radio calls. The squad's lights were on and his service revolver was snapped in its holster. He left a widow and two young children.

A $50,000 reward was offered for information leading to the arrest and conviction of Mork's killer.

Security guard Daniel Williams said he thought Iola Police Chief Michael Schertz looked tired when he arrived at the murder scene about 4 a.m. that morning. Schertz lifted a blanket to look at Mork's body, then shook his head.

The relationship had been rocky between the Iola chief and the dead officer. Schertz had planned a disciplinary hearing for Mork for the week after the car show. The charges related to Mork's confiscation of two twelve-packs of beer. At an earlier disciplinary hearing, Mork had been issued a letter of reprimand by the village board for law violations. The village police committee told Schertz he wasn't doing his job teaching the young officer police procedure.

Roger Miller, police chief of the town of St. Lawrence and a part-time Iola officer, said Schertz told him that if he couldn't get Mork to resign, "maybe (I) should just slit his throat and be done with him."

Miller said Schertz told him he had confiscated and thrown away a .380-caliber Baretta three years earlier. The gun matched what was believed to be the murder weapon.

Two weeks after the murder, Schertz said he had lied about destroying the weapon and that he had sold it and another gun, a .38-caliber Smith & Wesson snubnose, for $200 at an Appleton tavern.

Eleven days after Mork's murder, Schertz, who had served fourteen years on the department, was charged with misconduct over the gun sales. He also was charged with felony theft of two handguns and suspended indefinitely without pay.

A month later, Schertz was charged with first-degree murder and held at the Portage County jail in Stevens Point for killing Gerald Mork. The criminal complaint said Schertz repeatedly tried to fire Mork after he was hired over another applicant favored by Schertz.

A key witness against Schertz was Thomas Doerr, a cross-country trucker who was among the group of motorcyclists Mork had confronted at the Iola restaurant. Doerr would testify he saw Schertz driving toward the cemetery where Mork was murdered. The motorcyclists, who were hanging out at a village park, said they saw two squad cars driving to the cemetery. They said they heard two shots, then saw Schertz driving away.

Schertz took the witness stand in his own defense, denying he had killed Gerald Mork. Schertz's wife, Beverly, testified her husband was home in bed when witnesses said they heard shots fired in the vicinity of the cemetery about 4:20 a.m.

Two weeks before Christmas 1985, an Eau Claire County jury deliberated more than four hours before finding Schertz innocent of the murder of Gerald Mork. Schertz put his hands to his face and wept.

Later, he said the investigation that led to the murder charges against him was "the most unscrupulous, biased investigation I've ever seen in my entire law enforcement career."

District Attorney Thomas Maroney defended the murder investigation as "thorough and exhaustive."

Two days short of a year after Mork was murdered, Schertz was found innocent of gun theft charges. He filed a lawsuit against Waupaca County officials accusing them of trying to frame him for murder and sought reinstatement as Iola police chief. In March 1987, Outagamie Circuit Judge Michael Gage ruled that the firing of Schertz was justified.

Police reopened the investigation of Mork's murder, seeking new leads. But the case remains unsolved.

Did the jury make the right decision in acquitting Michael Schertz for the murder of Officer Gerald Mork? Were the motorcyclists who provided key testimony against Schertz involved in the murder?

13.
Who killed Linda Wegner?
La Crosse, 1988

The most distinguishing characteristic about Linda Wegner may have been her Boston accent. A quiet, mild-mannered woman, she often visited her parents back in Boston, but lived with her husband, Glenn, and one-year-old daughter, Jenny, in La Crosse.

She had worked for more than seven years as a nurse's aide at Bethany-St. Joseph Care Center, a nursing home. She also had worked as a nurse's aide in Massachusetts, where she was known as Linda Levesque during a previous marriage.

The Wegners had bought some land a year earlier,

where they had planted 130 trees and planned to build a new home someday.

On April 19, 1988, Wegner had the day off. She may have planned to spend the day organizing the secluded house on Zion Road where her family had moved a week earlier.

Glenn Wegner, a produce and dairy manager at a local grocery store, called his wife of four years about noon, but got no answer. When he arrived home about 5:30 p.m., he found her dead in the bathroom. Her throat had been slashed with a sharp object.

No weapon was recovered and there was no sign of a struggle or forced entry to the home. A blue, gray and white comforter was missing from the home along with a pair of bed sheets and Linda's purse. There was no sign that she was sexually assaulted and investigators found no link between her death and three unsolved sexual assaults on La Crosse's South Side.

Police questioned workers building condominiums down the hill from the Wegner home, but they hadn't heard anything. Investigators believe Linda Wegner was killed sometime before her husband called at noon.

The investigation centered on an unknown salesman for a driveway repair or sealcoating company who may have visited the Wegner home that morning. An older model pickup truck also was seen in the area. But detectives never identified the man or the truck.

Glenn Wegner, whose family lived in nearby Bangor, was provided solace by his brother, Greg, a grief counselor who had studied under Elizabeth Kubler-Ross, author of *On Death and Dying*.

But the distraught husband could never completely recover from the loss of his wife that day. Not only were investigators unable to find a suspect, they also could not establish a motive for the murder. Was Linda Wegner killed by a stranger that spring day or by someone she knew?

14.

Who stole Hercules Dousman's silver?

Prairie du Chien, 1981

When antique silverware, a tea set and other silver pieces were stolen in 1981 from a mansion at the Villa Louis State Historical Site at Prairie du Chien, the missing items had more than a monetary value.

A six-piece tea set also stolen was made in the 1850s by E. Jaccard Co. of St. Louis and bore the monogram HLD, which stood for Hercules Louis Dousman, Wisconsin's first millionaire.

Michael Douglass, museum curator, said the missing items were a national treasure.

"You could buy a comparable set on the market, but you could not replace the long family history," he said.

Dousman made his fortune in the fur trade. He started with a small job in Green Bay and in 1826 went to Prairie du Chien to become agent for the American Fur Company. Within a decade, he became one of the richest men in the state. In 1836, he bought Black Hawk, known as the fastest horse in the Old Northwest, and built a race track next to his opulent mansion. Dousman also had bought up much of the property in Prairie du Chien and sold it at a substantial profit. Later, he invested in sawmills and steamboats.

Eighteen years after the burglary, FBI agents recovered

two pieces of flatware and 17 pieces of hollowware pitchers, bowls, platters and candlesticks somewhere in Texas. Assisted by the Texas Rangers and the Texas fire marshal's office, the agents also found the stolen tea set.

But some of the silver still is missing and the thief has not been identified.

15.

Who killed Father Alfred Kunz?

Dane, 1998

Father Alfred Kunz was known for cooking a great fish fry on Friday nights. A parish priest for thirty-one years in a small village of northern Dane County, he also preserved the church's traditions and people came from miles around to hear him celebrate Mass in Latin.

About 10 p.m. on March 3, 1998, Father Charles Fiore dropped him off at St. Michael's Catholic Church in Dane after they had taped a radio show in Monroe. It was the last time anyone saw Father Kunz alive. He was found the next morning with his throat cut.

Who would viciously murder the kindly 67-year-old priest?

Investigators were hampered by the fact that Kunz didn't have a secretary and kept no daily schedule. They questioned parishioners and village residents.

At first, they focused on Kunz' conservative views. Perhaps the priest had offended someone who had come to him with a problem. An FBI profile described the probable killer as someone who knew Kunz and who may live in the village.

Three months after the murder, investigators checked

out an anonymous letter that was harshly critical of Father Kunz. The letter had been sent to an Episcopal priest in Baraboo.

But the letter didn't lead to the killer and, after more than two thousand interviews and five hundred tips, the investigation failed to turn up any solid leads.

In November 1999, one-and-a-half years after the slaying, Dane County Sheriff Gary Hamblin held a community meeting in the village of Dane to quash rumors and try to generate new leads. Tip sheets were passed out to about one-hundred fifty people who attended the meeting.

Hamblin told the crowd that Kunz was not stabbed once for each year of his age, as had been rumored, and that he was not mutilated. The sheriff said the killer probably had a personal dispute with the priest and wasn't a serial killer or someone just passing through the village.

In early 2000, investigators thought that perhaps Kunz was murdered by a serial killer when Monsignor Thomas Wells, a 56-year-old priest in Germantown, Maryland, was stabbed to death. But a local homeless man was arrested for the Maryland murder and detectives doubt the stabbing of Monsignor Wells was linked to the Kunz case.

Another anonymous letter named a suspect, but detectives ruled out that person after checking it out.

Two years after the killing of Father Kunz, Hamblin delivered a bombshell. He said there was some evidence that the priest had a history of "intimate relationships with adult women" and that the killer could have been a jealous husband or lover.

"I think everybody in town knew that Kunz had female friends, and didn't think anything of it," Dane Village President David Wipperfurth told the *The Capital Times*. "I mean, it wasn't as if he was running around every night or anything crazy like that. But yeah, he was human."

The sheriff's bombshell spurred outrage among parishioners, village residents and Kunz' fellow priests. Hamblin said he received hostile letters, e-mail messages and phone calls. He also received more tips about the possible killer.

The Rev. Lawrence Brey, who lived with Father Kunz for six months before the murder while recovering from heart bypass surgery, said he never saw a sign that the priest was involved in an intimate relationship.

But Brey had his own theory about the murder. He told Rob Zaleski of *The Capital Times* that he believed Father Kunz was killed by a hit man hired by officials of the Catholic Church.

Father Alfred Kunz

Brey said Father Kunz knew about "evil situations" involving other priests at various midwestern parishes and church officials wanted him silenced.

Another theory was that the priest was murdered by a Satanic cult and linked to exorcisms that Father Kunz had performed.

Both Brey's theory and the cult theory were discounted by the Madison Diocese.

Did a disgruntled parishioner kill Father Kunz, perhaps angered by his conservative views? Was it a spurned lover or jealous boyfriend or husband? Or was it a hit man or Satanic cult?

Theories abound and, so far, investigators haven't been able to identify the killer.

16.

Who killed Sheldon Kliman?

Spooner, 1986

Sheldon Kliman was a man of habit and every morning he followed the same routine. He unlocked his Spooner movie theater, then went across the street for breakfast. He then returned to the theater to clean up for the that day's shows.

Kliman, 59, was a ventriloquist, ex-vaudvillian and popular owner of Spooner's Palace Theater.

As a youngster, he had appeared with his father in a vaudeville act. He later continued his act under the stage name of Shelly Kelly. He still performed, mostly for charity groups, after moving to Spooner in 1966.

"I would have thought he didn't have an enemy in the world," said his friend, attorney Woodrow Bitney.

On a Monday morning in June 1986, Kliman opened up the theater as he usually did, then walked across the street for sweet rolls and coffee. He brought his breakfast back to the theater about 8:15 a.m.

Twenty minutes later, Kliman's son, Irwin, 22, found his father's body lying in the theater doorway. He had been stabbed eight times.

Two people were questioned about the murder but released. A pair of knives were found but police said they weren't used in the murder.

Five months after the vicious stabbing in broad daylight, police were running out of hope they would ever catch the killer.

"Right now, we're at a dead end," said police Sgt. David LaPorte. "I really think we've got a lost cause here. Everything we get back from the crime lab is negative."

17.
Who killed
Marshal William Gibson?
Horicon, 1882

When a stranger came to town on Oct. 20, 1882, he went almost immediately to the American House, where he began drinking. The man got so drunk that Charles Herker, a saloon keeper, had to put him to bed.

When he awoke about 5 p.m., the man went back to the tavern and picked up where he'd left off. Three hours later, he'd become so drunk and unruly that police were called to take him away.

Marshal William Gibson and Julius Winnefeld escorted the man to jail. A revolver was taken from his right hip pocket and the man went to the jail without resistance. When the three men reached the lockup, Gibson let go of the man to unlock the door. At that point, the man pulled out a second .40-caliber bulldog revolver with his left hand and fired a single shot at Gibson.

The shot struck Gibson at close range just above his left ear, taking off part of his ear and penetrating his brain. The man then turned to shoot Winnefeld, who still held him by the right arm. Winnefeld grabbed the revolver and wrestled the man to subdue him. But the man, apparently not as drunk as the two law officers had thought, managed to escape.

Winnefeld raised an alarm and the murderer might have been quickly caught if not for another incident. A fire had broken out at the blacksmith shop of Van Brunt & Davis Co., a cedar manufacturing firm. The whole town became absorbed by the fire, and didn't pay any attention to the fact that the marshal lay dying from a gunshot wound and a killer was on the loose.

"The cry of murder could not be heard," the *Beaver Dam Argus* reported. "Men, women and children rushing by near the man (Gibson), who lay in an insensible condition with his brains oozing from an ugly wound."

Gibson finally received medical attention an hour later, but it was far too late. He was in such bad condition that he didn't survive.

Within two hours, every farmer for several miles around Horicon was provided a description of the deadly stranger and asked to watch for him.

"There was intense excitement and the expressions made by the crowd leave little doubt that had the man been captured last night he would have been strung to the nearest tree," the newspaper said. "Never since the time of the Indian scare in 1861, which is known in the *History of Dodge County* as the Horicon War, has there been such excitement in the village."

Some residents suspected the killer had murdered a Waupaca man earlier and robbed a bank. They believed he shot Gibson to avoid being linked to those crimes.

But the killer of Marshal William Gibson never was brought to justice.

18.

Why was her ring found on the ice?

Muskego, 1961

They were celebrating the new year — six young people out for a ride on January 2, 1961. Earlier that day, they had driven out on Little Muskego Lake, where driver Dale Olson, 20, spun the car on the ice.

Olson and his two companions, Jerry Hammernik, 18, and Roger Holtz, 20, had driven Hammernik's sister, Jean Marie, 20, and her two girlfriends, Helen Destrampe, 17, and Korinne Wellner, 19, to the lake so the young women could go skating.

When they got to the lake, however, the young women decided it was more fun riding in the car on the ice. Olson and the driver of another car would get the speed up to 35 to 40 mph, then slam on the brakes and send their cars spinning wildly.

"You go ice skating and we won't come back after you," one of the young men said.

They left the lake about 5:30 pm., after about an hour of driving around on it. The young people bought two six-packs of beer and each drank a can. They drove back to the lake about 6 p.m.

Holtz later would deny that Olson spun the car on the second trip to the lake. But a half hour later, the car suddenly plunged through the ice.

Olson later said he frantically tried to open the driver's side door as the car submerged in the icy water, but it wouldn't budge. He rolled down the window.

"I felt someone pushing me and I reached back and grabbed them," he told the *Waukesha Freeman.* "The next thing I knew I was free from the car and coming to the surface."

When Jean Hammernik, who was in the front seat with Olson, rolled down the passenger side window, Holtz, who was in the back seat with the three others, said he was able to swim out and reach the surface.

The three young women were not so lucky. The bodies of Jean Hammernik and Helen Destrampe were recovered by diver Russell Jacobs of Brookfield. Korinne Wellner's body wasn't recovered until two days later.

Korinne's arms had become entangled in her jacket, perhaps as she tried to take it off in a desperate effort to swim to the surface.

It seemed a simple but tragic case of young people dying after they got involved in a dangerous activity. But there was one bizarre aspect to the case.

Korinne's class ring was found on the ice, not in the water. Had Korinne actually made it to the surface and grabbed the ice to pull herself from the frigid water? Or was one of the young men wearing her ring? Why did the three young men live while the three young women died?

Jerome Hammernik, the father of Jean and Jerry, said his son had to be restrained from diving back into the water to rescue the young women.

"Those boys did their best to get the girls out, I'm satisfied of that," he said.

19.

Was the Walker House haunted?

Mineral Point, 1978

The Walker House, Wisconsin's oldest inn, opened in 1836 in the mining town of Mineral Point in south western Wisconsin. Six years later, the inn was the scene of a hanging that some believe caused a ghost to inhabit the inn more than a century later.

On November 1, 1842, four thousand people came to watch William Caffee hung from a tree outside the inn. Many families camped on hillsides on the outskirts of town. Caffee, an unrepentant killer, was convicted of shooting Samuel Southwick to death.

Not only did Caffee show no remorse, he also displayed a nonchalant attitude toward his own death. He used two beer bottles to beat out a macabre funeral march while sitting astride his casket, according to an account in *Haunted Heartland* by Beth Scott and Michael Norman.

In the early 1970s, the Walker House was reopened after several years of refurbishing that followed decades of neglect. But the business failed and was sold in 1978 to Dr. David Ruf of Darlington.

When Ruf bought the building, a student from Madison living in a second-floor apartment complained he was kept awake by the constant turning of the doorknob on the door to his bedroom.

Walker Calvert was hired by Ruf to manage the inn and he also noticed strange happenings. A wooden door that covered water pipes repeatedly flew open, usually when diners were in the restaurant in the late afternoon. Calvert sometimes would find himself talking to someone when the room was empty, and the clanging of pots and pans often were heard in the kitchen when no one was there. Employees also heard the sound of heavy breathing and footsteps.

In 1981, Calvert went out to a second-floor porch and saw a headless old man sitting on a bench. The ghost wore a gray miner's jacket and blue jeans. A few days later, a waitress saw the ghost of a young man who stood beside her for an instant, then disappeared.

Calvert came to believe that the ghost was the incarnation of William Caffee, the condemned man from 140 years earlier. Calvert believed the ghost didn't mean any harm, but was upset by large groups of diners at the inn because of the crowd that had gathered to watch his execution.

20.
Who stabbed and killed Hazel Williams?
Madison, 1960

Hazel Williams, 50, was a widow who lived with her mother on Center Avenue on Madison's East Side. A few days before Christmas on Dec. 20, 1960, a man came to the door about 6 p.m. wanting to rent an apartment from the two women.

A short time later, the man returned to the women's house alone, telling Williams' mother, Frances Gallagher, 78, that he wanted money, not a room.

"Are you crazy?" Gallagher asked him. Then he hit her, knocking her to the floor.

The prospective renter turned out to be a vicious killer who stabbed Hazel Williams forty to fifty times in the chest and head, probably with an old-fashioned hat pin, and left her body in a bathtub at the empty apartment. Then he returned to where the women lived a few doors away and beat Hazel's mother within an inch of her life. The six-foot-tall man, who wore a gray tweed coat with flecks of red, fled with Gallagher's purse, which contained about $150.

Besides the stab wounds, cigarette burns would found on Williams' shoulders and chest. Police believed the killer burned her to try to get her to tell him where her mother kept the money.

Neighbors saw Gallagher coming home from the store with a bag of groceries about 5:30 p.m., but when a television repairman knocked on the door about 6:45 p.m., he got no answer.

Gallagher was found lying on the kitchen floor by her granddaughter about 4 p.m. the next day, nearly twenty-four hours after the beating. The temperature in the house had dropped to about 40 degrees because no one was tending the furnace. The 22-year-old granddaughter thought her grandmother had been injured in a fall and called an ambulance. Six hours later, when Gallagher regained consciousness, she told about the beating and her daughter's body was found.

A broken piece of metal about two inches long was embedded in the back of Gallagher's head. She also suffered a fractured skull and broken collarbone along with cuts and bruises. A guard was placed on her hospital room. She barely survived the brutal attack, and two months later she was placed in a nursing home.

The seemingly unprovoked attack on the two women aroused fear and outrage throughout the city. A headline in the *Wisconsin State Journal* proclaimed: "Police seek 'maniac' for murder in city."

"He must have been a madman because only a maniac would inflict the wounds these two women suffered," coroner Michael Malloy told *State Journal* reporter June Dieckmann.

An acquaintance of Williams was questioned after police found his phone number on a pad in the women's home.

A week before the attack, Gallagher's name had made the

Frances Gallagher

newspapers due to criticism about the condition of her five apartment houses along Center Avenue. A city board of review granted property tax reductions to a dozen neighboring property owners who said their properties were devalued by the deteriorating condition of Gallagher's apartments.

Was the killer seeking revenge on a slum landlord? Or did he read about Gallagher in the newspaper and target her as an easy mark for robbery? The case never was solved.

21.
What happened to the Krnaks?

Fort Atkinson, 1998

How does a family disappear without a trace? That's a question that has perplexed investigators since Allen Krnak, 55, his wife, Donna, 52, and their son, Thomas, 29, left with their dog on July 2,

1998, for the family cabin near Coloma in Waushara County. The family from Helenville, in Jefferson County, was never seen again.

"We have nothing new to go on," Jefferson County Sheriff Orval Quamme told *Wisconsin State Journal* reporter Richard Jaeger two years after the disappearance. "The calls are fewer and fewer which means this thing is growing cold."

The Krnak's oldest son, Andrew, 30, has been viewed as the prime suspect in his family's disappearance. He changed his name to Derek Nicholas Anderson a few days after his parents and brother vanished.

He was convicted of using false names and social security numbers to obtain $87,832 in college educational grants and sentenced to 17 months in federal prison.

But the former Andrew Krnak has repeatedly denied any involvement in the disappearance. He stopped cooperating with detectives and retracted an offer to take a lie detector test on the advice of his attorney.

Although there is no evidence against him, the former Krnak was the last to see his family alive. He waited five days before calling authorities and, instead of contacting police, called a game warden in Sauk County where the family's pickup truck was found abandoned near a trout

Allen, Donna and Thomas Krnak

stream they often visited near Reedsburg.

The pickup truck yielded no evidence other than fingerprints of family members. There was no blood or signs of a struggle. Dogs and all-terrain vehicles were used to search the area where the truck was found but the search also uncovered no clues.

In June 1999, divers also searched Mason Lake in Adams County after an ice fisherman snagged human hair on his line. Relatives of the Krnak family have a cabin on the lake but this search also turned up nothing.

Relatives from the Milwaukee area put up a $10,000 reward and distributed posters asking for information at campgrounds, gas stations and roadside restaurants. They hoped someone would come forward with new information about the family.

Still, the key to solving the case could remain with the former Andrew Krnak, who isn't talking.

22.
Who killed Donna Mraz?
Madison, 1982

Donna Mraz, 19, was on her way home from a waitress job at restaurant on Madison's State Street when she was brutally stabbed outside Camp Randall Stadium on the University of Wisconsin campus.

Witnesses heard her screams and came to her rescue, only to see her assailant slipping quietly into the shadows. One witness, who saw the victim collapse from his apartment window, was asked to undergo hypnosis to see if he could recall other details. The case was eerily reminiscent of the Christine Rothschild murder more than a decade earlier and, like the Rothschild case, offered few

Donna Mraz

clues.

Because of the apparently random selection of the victim, the murder terrified female students on the Madison campus. The city council considered beefing up late-night bus service.

Donna Mraz was a junior studying business. Her family lived in Delavan.

Police compiled a composite sketch of a bearded man seen near the stadium and a $10,000 reward was offered. A pair of blue jeans found draped over a tree were tested to determine if dark stains on them were blood. Crime lab tests determined the jeans had blood on them, but it was from a rabbit.

Two years afterward, the victim's body was exhumed to compare her teeth to bite marks on a possible suspect in prison. No arrest was made and the suspect later died.

In July 1985, the fatal stabbing of a Marquette University student was strikingly similar to the Mraz case. Antoinette Reardon, 20, of Kirkwood, Missouri, died about three hours after she was stabbed near the campus. A man with past convictions for sexual assault and armed robbery was arrested, but could not be linked to the Mraz murder.

23.
Who killed Albert Buehl?
Janesville, 1969

Victor Munro thought there was something suspicious about the fact that the Cronin-Hovland Liquor Store in Janesville was unlocked and no one was around.

Munro worked across the street as a refrigerator repairman at Phil's Refrigeration Service and decided to stop in the liquor store on the morning of June 16, 1969, to check on an ice-making machine his boss had repaired the day before.

"I thought someone might be loading beer into the cooler, so I looked in there, and there he was lying between two rows of beer," Munro told the *Wisconsin State Journal*.

The victim was Albert Buehl, 62, who had opened the store at 8 a.m. as he had done for two years. He was hit with two blasts from a shotgun and probably already dead, but Munro rushed to the phone and called for police and an ambulance.

If Buehl opened the store at 8 a.m. and Munro arrived 16 minutes later, it's amazing he didn't bump into the killer. Despite the fresh evidence and quick response, the case has remained unsolved for more than three decades.

24.
Who murdered Kelly Drew and Timothy Hack?

Concord, 1980

When Kelly Drew and Timothy Hack didn't show up for Mass on Aug. 10, 1980, some people wondered whether they'd eloped. That hope, however, was quickly dashed when Hack's car was found parked outside a dance hall. His wallet with sixty-five dollars in cash and his checkbook were found inside.

The night before, the couple had attended a wedding dance at the Concord Recreation Center in the Jefferson County hamlet of Concord, just off Interstate 94.

Kelly Drew graduated from the Janesville Academy of Beauty Culture two months earlier and was working at Brothers II styling salon in Fort Atkinson. She also worked part-time at a Dairy Queen restaurant. Tim Hack was a champion in tractor-pulling contests who worked on the family farm near Hebron. Both were religious and Drew had taught Sunday school as a child to younger children on her block.

The families of the missing couple recruited about a hundred volunteers to comb the rural area near Concord. The Jefferson County Sheriff's Department checked campsites and waded through marshland. A reward fund of two thousand dollars later grew to ten thousand dollars, but it went unclaimed.

The case turned ominous when Kelly Drew's purse and clothing were found scattered along a rural road between Concord and Farmington.

David and Pat Hack, left, Timothy's parents, join Kelly's parents, Norma and Gerald Walker, in presenting a poster they hoped would locate the missing teenagers.

On October 19, Harmon Banks and Willie McClendon, both of Milwaukee, were hunting squirrels along Hutisford Road near Ixonia when they went into the woods on the Donald Schmidt farm. They spotted the nude, decomposing body of a young woman. The body was identified as Kelly Drew. The following morning, state agents searching the area found Hack's body in a cornfield about a hundred feet north of where Drew was found.

The bodies were so badly decomposed that it was impossible to determine how they died, although investigators believed Drew was sexually assaulted.

Two years after the murders, the former wife of a convicted child molester showed investigators maps with a small red devil drawn in the margin. The devil's tail supposedly pointed to the location where the bodies of Hack and Drew were found.

The woman said her former husband participated in

black masses and witchcraft. Besides Hack and Drew, she said the cult was responsible for the drowning death of two-year-old Michelle Manders of Watertown in 1981, as well as the 1979 murder of Jay Kelly Flom of Milwaukee, and the 1974 murder of Catherine Sjoberg of Oconomowoc, who had disappeared six years earlier from the same dance hall.

The satanic cult theory, popularized by Milwaukee private detective Norbert Kutczewski, quickly was unraveled by investigators. The map had no devil drawings, but had penciled circles which they believed were locations of jobs where the woman's ex-husband had worked as a painter.

Police questioned suspects in other murder cases, including Henry Lee Lucas, who confessed to hundreds of murders from his Texas prison cell and later recanted those confessions.

The 1984 murder of a Waukegan, Illinois, woman had striking similarities to the Drew-Hack case. A pair of killers shot the Waukegan woman's male companion, dragged her from a parking lot, raped and murdered her, and later dumped her body in Wisconsin. Detectives questioned Hector Reuben Sanchez and Warren Peters of Zion, Illinois, who were convicted of that murder, but they couldn't prove Sanchez and Peters had been in Jefferson County.

Although the killer's trail has grown cold, Drew and Hack haven't been forgotten in Jefferson County, where scholarships were established a year after their murders — the Kelly Drew Beauty Culture Scholarship and the Tim Hack Agricultural Award.

25.
Who killed Ophelia Preston?
Milwaukee, 1994

Ophelia Preston's body was found in a garbage cart in 1994, in the 1700 block of King Drive on Milwaukee's North Side. She had been strangled.

A city worker whose telephone number was found in Preston's pocket was questioned in her murder. He said he knew her from a cocaine recovery group and admitted having sex with her three days before she died.

Preston, a crack addict, was among a dozen women strangled in the same area during the decade. The man said he "dope dated" Preston, which means he exchanged drugs for sex. He also had been trained in knot-tying and at least four of the women were strangled with rope or clothesline.

Some of the women were strangled with the killer's bare hands. Others, like Preston, were strangled with rope. George L. "Mule" Jones pleaded guilty to one murder and was suspected of several others.

But the city worker questioned in Preston's death never was charged.

26.
Was Edward Kanieski guilty of murder?
Wisconsin Rapids, 1952

The almost nude body of Cad Bates was found on a hot summer day June 30, 1952, in her bedroom behind the tavern she operated near Kellner, not far from Wisconsin Rapids. Bates was wearing only her shoes and stockings. The bedroom was orderly and two wine glasses were on a bedside table next to a nearly empty bottle of Christian Brothers brandy. A blood-soaked towel was wrapped around the woman's neck and a chenille rug was on the bed. Under the towel, a cord had been fastened tightly around her neck. Her skull also had been crushed with a heavy object.

Cad Bates, 76, had operated the tavern near the Wood-Portage county line for five years. Her tavern had a reputation as a sporting place, where Cad was happy to supply her male customers with prostitutes. In back, where she lived, Cad also let her sporting customers use the bedrooms.

Edward Kanieski, a jackhammer operator, found Cad's body when he stopped at the tavern for a drink while taking a ride with his wife and young son, Eddie Jr.

His presence when the body was found didn't look good for Kanieski. In 1950, he had been sentenced to one to two years in prison for breaking and entering a town of Saratoga home. He had cut the telephone wires and forced his way into the house, where he was shot in the neck by the victim, Linda Eberius. On the Fourth of July, five days after Cad's body was found, Kanieski was arrested for the rape of a ten-year-old Grand Rapids girl.

Then detectives learned Kanieski wasn't at all unfamiliar with Cad's Tavern and the slain proprietor. In fact, he knew her well. He had been to the tavern several times during the previous three months, even spending time with a woman there once or twice. He had told Cad Bates he was an aviator, working as a crop duster at nearby cranberry marshes. He promised to fly Cad to Iowa, where she wanted to visit relatives. A few weeks before the murder, he'd shown up at the tavern with a bandage on his head, the result of a fall outside a funeral home. But Kanieski told Cad he'd been injured in an airplane accident.

At first, Kanieski denied he'd been to the tavern on the Saturday night of June 28, two days before the body was found. After several witnesses placed him there, he admitted the truth – that he'd stopped by for a drink. Kanieski talked to Cad Bates awhile before he left. After he was gone, patrons said Cad appeared agitated and upset. She began clearing glasses away and said she was tired and wanted to close up early.

Edward Kanieski

When police asked Kanieski about scratches on his arms, he said he got them from picking blueberries. Were they actually from a death struggle with Cad Bates? Detectives seized Kanieski's black oxford shoes as evidence. They had recently been resoled, but, when the new soles were ripped off, no blood was found. But Kanieski was charged with the murder of Cad Bates.

The key to the prosecution's case against Kanieski was built on the new science of microscopic fiber examination by the Wisconsin Crime Lab. Crime lab expert Laurin Goin repeatedly took the witness stand, connecting Kanieski to the crime through similarities between the hair from one of Cad's dogs and one found on his jacket, between fibers taken from his purple wool trousers and those found on the chenille rug and among the fibers of the rope about the victim's neck. Kanieski submitted a sample of pubic hair and Goin found an apparent match there, too.

The jury deliberated six-and-a-half hours before finding Kanieski guilty of the murder. He served his life sentence at Waupun State Prison and later at Fox Lake Correctional Institution. He steadfastly maintained his innocence through the years and appealed the case six times to state and federal courts.

Six times his appeals were rejected and Kanieski later said he was denied parole because he wouldn't admit to the murder. During the fall of 1971, he suffered a heart attack and was hospitalized at University Hospital in Madison, where he underwent open heart surgery in December of that year.

Three months later, his conviction was overturned by the Wisconsin Supreme Court. He had served nineteen years in prison. Writing for the court's majority, Justice Horace Wilkie said the circumstantial case against Kanieski didn't justify a conviction. He also rejected the microscopic fiber evidence.

"We find that the only established fact is that defendant (Kanieski) took forty minutes too long in getting home. There is no fact to support the proposition that he went back to the Bates tavern, that he had some reason to kill Miss Bates or that he committed the crime."

Kanieski died in April 1975 and, after his death, his son, Eddie Jr., set out to prove his innocence. The younger Kanieski, who had been with his father that day a quarter century earlier when the body of Cad Bates was found, wrote letters to major figures in the case and searched court records. His efforts were complicated by the fact that Eddie Kanieski Jr. is blind from an eye disease he has had since shortly after birth. His wife, Colleen, had to read court documents to him, and he had to be driven to interviews.

The Kanieski case, along with that of Kenny Ray Reichhoff, prompted the state to change its innocent convicts compensation law in 1980. Gov. Lee Dreyfus signed legislation that said convicts later found innocent need only provide clear and convincing evidence rather than proving innocence beyond a reasonable doubt. The new law also increased the amount of compensation.

In *The Tangled Web,* a 1993 book by John Potter, the Wood County district attorney who had prosecuted Kanieski, Potter concluded not only that Kanieski was guilty of the Bates murder, but that he would have gone on to become a serial killer if he hadn't been stopped.

Two years later, a book called *Please Pass the Roses* by Colleen Kohler Kanieski, the wife of Eddie Jr., professed the elder Kanieski's innocence, while highlighting her husband's struggles with blindness and his father's imprisonment.

Did Edward Kanieski Sr. kill Cad Bates as the crime lab evidence purported to show in 1952? Or did his prior record and evasiveness about frequenting the tavern make him an easy scapegoat?

27.
Who killed Chad Maurer?
Madison, 1990

The picture of Chad Maurer that ran every year during the 1990s in the classified ads of Wisconsin newspapers showed a vigorous, handsome young man with striking blond hair.

He didn't look like a youth who would be found dead inside a car parked in a garage on Chicago's South Side.

Chicago police quickly ruled the death in May 1990 of Maurer, 21, of Madison, a suicide. But his parents, John and Dolly Maurer, couldn't believe their son would kill himself and later police began to investigate the case as murder.

Every year on the anniversary of his death, the Maurers ran a classified ad with their son's picture. That ad urged anyone with information about his death to come forward.

The case was featured on the television show "Unsolved Mysteries" and the Maurers lobbied legislators, wrote letters and made phone calls in their effort to keep the investigation going.

Maurer was athletic and liked skateboarding, snowboarding and racing dirt bikes. He was a dirt-bike champion and collected a lot of trophies.

He also had smoked marijuana and used LSD. Police said his presence on Chicago's South Side and his death may have been related to drugs.

On Saturday, May 17, 1990, Maurer came home for lunch from his new job at the Village Pedaler, a bicycle shop where he had started working two days earlier. He made some sandwiches and told his mother he was going back to work.

Two days later, Maurer's body was found in a high-crime area of Chicago.

When Maurer was killed, Madison's South Side had a growing gang and drug presence; and youths from Chicago's South Side had moved into the area, not far from the Maurers' home.

Police identified three suspects who had recently moved from Chicago to Madison. One of them was arrested and sentenced to 27 years in prison for another crime.

In February 1998, the Maurers were asked to provide blood samples to compare with blood found at the crime scene. Those samples would be used to determine whether blood found on Maurer's clothes belonged to him or the killer. But after they provided the samples, the Maurers heard nothing more from the police.

The Maurers were angry at Chicago police and believe they were negligent about protecting the crime scene, possibly because of the early ruling that the death was a suicide. A jacket, for example, that didn't belong to Maurer was seen in a crime scene photo, but later disappeared.

"Chicago was as criminally negligent as the criminals in this case," Dolly Maurer told an Associated Press reporter in 1992. "Our love for Chad just keeps us going, and all of our good memories."

Did Chad Maurer die because he was involved in a drug deal gone bad? Or was he abducted by gang members, taken to Chicago and killed? His parents still want answers.

28.
What happened to Robert Christian?

Baraboo, 1977

Robert Christian, 18, left his home on Madison's East Side to go bow hunting with a friend near Baraboo. But he never returned and that day, Sept. 16, 1977, was the last anyone heard of him.

The young man left home about 5:30 p.m. and was scheduled to meet Randy Griffith at Griffith's home near Baraboo.

"It's like the Earth opened up and swallowed him," Carrie Christian, told a *Wisconsin State Journal* reporter nearly a decade after her son disappeared.

When Carrie Christian returned from a high school football game with her two youngest children, she got a call from Griffith's mother that Robert never arrived. Robert's mother called the police to report him missing.

The Christian family car, which Robert had been driving, was found abandoned with the battery, license plate, hubcaps and wheels missing. Those hubcaps and wheels, punctured by bullet holes, were found a week later in a dump near the Badger Army Ammunition Plant. But detectives said the bullet holes could have come from someone using the hubcaps and wheels for target practice after they were discarded.

"I think he's buried somewhere and not in Sauk County," said then-sheriff Alan Shanks. "I believe someone abducted him where the car was found and took him somewhere else and killed him."

The Christian family hired a private detective and consulted two psychics. One of the psychics said he believed Robert picked up two people, an Asian woman and a man in a fatigue jacket. She also saw a sign that said "Baraboo - - 12 miles" and said the three people stopped at a place with a horseshoe-shaped counter. She said she saw the three people enter a white house, where Robert was hurt.

Another psychic reported seeing a low, brown building, a road sign with the name "South Shore Drive" and drugs.

Carrie Christian said her family located a road called South Shore Drive, where they also found a white cottage that later was torn down.

Someone reported seeing Robert Christian in Canada in 1985 and investigators checked out other leads in

Florida, Montana and New York, where skeletal remains were found. None of the leads unraveled the mystery.

The disappearance of their son wouldn't be the last tragedy to befall the Christian family. In March 1983, their oldest daughter, Kathy, died in a fire at Rosa's Cantina near Stoughton. Three members of the Ghost Riders motor- cycle gang were convicted of Kathy Christian's murder.

The motorcycle gang probably wasn't linked to Robert Christian's disappearance. Is he dead or alive?

29.

Are there man-made pyramids in Rock Lake?

Lake Mills, 2000 B.C.

Rock formations are common in Wisconsin, mostly caused by glaciers that swept across the land. Beneath 45 feet of water in Rock Lake, near Lake Mills, are pyramids fashioned of rocks that appear ce- mented together and man-made. Experts believe the pyra- mids date back as far as 2000 B.C.

Over the years, people have offered various theories about how the pyramids got there. Lloyd Hornbostel of Beloit, who owned property on the lake, said he believed they're related to ancient copper trade routes. The lake is on one of the southern trade routes from Isle Royale in Lake Superior.

Historians found evidence of food storage and copper pits around the lake and have searched for copper arti- facts under water.

"The pyramids are at a level that the lake was around 1200 to 2000 B.C.," Hornbostel told the *Wisconsin State Journal* in 1990. "This was the peak of copper mining activity. This is a very significant bit of work here."

If Hornbostel is correct about the origin, what did the pyramids mean? What was their significance to the ancient Native American culture?

A problem in investigating the pyramids is that the water is clear enough for good visibility for only about two weeks each spring after the ice melts and before algae and aquatic vegetation takes over the lake.

Wayne May and author Frank Joseph made several dives to explore the pyramids and determined that the uniformity and straight sides clearly indicate they were man-made.

"It's so perfectly shaped," May told the *Wisconsin State Journal*. "There's no way a glacier set this down. It looks like an altar."

One diver found a small animal bone along the lake bottom.

Some naturalists and archaeologists discount the claim that the rock formations are pyramids or man-made. They say the origin probably is natural and the rest is imagination.

But Joseph said he believes the structures verify that a human civilization existed in Wisconsin long ago.

30.

Who killed Barbara Blackstone?

Lyndon Station, 1987

Barbara Blackstone was a tall, popular teacher at New Lisbon High School. She and her husband, Tom, had built their isolated home near Lyndon Station themselves.

In early July 1987, Barbara Blackstone was mowing the

huge expanse of lawn near her rural home for a family picnic. She went to buy gasoline from a service station near Interstate 90-94 in Lyndon Station, then apparently returned home. Her car was found near a metal shed with her keys and purse still in it and the gas can in the trunk. But Barbara was nowhere to be found.

Barbara Blackstone

"The worst part of the whole thing is just sitting here waiting," said Herbert Fisher, Blackstone's wheelchair-bound father. "Maybe she's lying out in the woods dead or something."

Fisher's words were prophetic for Barbara Blackstone's decomposed body was found August 5 near Blanchardville in Lafayette County, not far from Argyle, where she grew up.

The Blackstone murder, along with area murders of two other women that summer, caused a panic in central Wisconsin that a serial killer was on the loose. The Guardian Angels, a New York City vigilante group, came to Wisconsin Dells to teach women how to protect themselves.

Kim Brown was convicted of the murder of Linda Nachreiner of rural Adams County and Terry Vollbrecht was convicted of murdering Angela Hackl of Lone Rock near Sauk City. But the Blackstone case remained unsolved.

Blackstone's husband, Tom, who circulated a poster and offered a reward before his wife's body was found, was a suspect. He wasn't as outgoing as his popular wife and may have resented the friendships she made with other teachers. But he had been working at his lawn service job the day she disappeared.

Fisher said he believed money was the motive. He said his daughter had a certificate of deposit at an Argyle bank and she may have told her abductors about it, hoping to escape during the long drive from Lyndon Station.

Fisher remained obsessed and saddened about the murder until his death several years later. Tom Blackstone returned to Ohio, where he had grown up. Barbara's mother, Lois Fisher, died in October 2000.

"I still miss her; I always will," Herbert Fisher said a year after that summer of terror. "It always seems like the good people get the dirty end of the stick."

31.

Who killed Officer Antonio Pingitore?

Kenosha, 1919

Three men shot and killed Kenosha Officer Antonio Pingitore after pulling off one of the most daring heists in the city's history.

On March 30, 1919, the masked men bound and gagged night watchman John Miller, then blew open and searched the vaults of the American Brass Company. They escaped with fifty thousand dollars in cash and bonds.

The men left the company's office shortly after midnight. A half hour later, they were trying to get gasoline to make their escape in a stolen car when they were confronted by Pingitore. After shooting and killing him, the men left in the stolen car, which was found in a ditch three miles west of Burlington.

Police arrested three men for the murder, but they turned out to be the wrong ones. After a massive manhunt, the men were taken into custody at McHenry, Illinois. They vehemently denied being involved in the theft and murder, and produced papers showing they worked for the government helping to eradicate barberry bushes. They recently had been discharged from the U.S. Army.

While police were busy detaining the wrong suspects, the killers fled with their substantial robbery proceeds and never were brought to justice. Early the next morning, police received word that three men with suitcases boarded a train at Lake Geneva bound for Chicago.

Pingitore had eleven hundred dollars in his pockets when he was killed, but the killers didn't stop to rob him. Pinkerton detectives were brought in to assist with the cases and investigators lifted fingerprints of the robbers left behind on a flashlight.

Expert safecrackers said the robbers appeared to be amateurs at breaking into safes. They tried to drill open the door of a safe and didn't come within a foot of the lock.

32.

Who shot and killed Helen Asmuth?

Neenah, 1984

Gunshots rang out July 31, 1984, at the 20-room home of James and Helen Asmuth in the upscale Doty Island neighborhood near Neenah along the Lake Winnebago shore.

A masked intruder burst into the Asmuth home. In the living room, he shot Asmuth, 64, a Fox Valley industrialist, in the stomach, then tied Helen's hands behind her back and led her outside. Asmuth followed the intruder and his wife outside and watched as she was shot to death.

Asmuth, the president of Wisconsin Tissue Mills, went back inside and called police.

Detectives theorized the murder probably was the result of a botched kidnapping attempt. But no suspects ever were identified.

Asmuth was the only person to see the intruder, described as white, in his early 30s, 6 feet tall with a heavy build. The murder weapon, believed to be a .38-caliber revolver, has not been found.

A $25,000 reward was offered by the parent company of Wisconsin Tissue. Investigators processed hundreds of leads and small pieces of information, but failed to solve the puzzling case.

A grand jury hearing in May 1993 gathered some evidence but failed to point to the killer.

"We're not overly concerned with the passage of time," Winnebago County Deputy District Attorney Vince Biskupic said in 1994. "Often the passage of time can turn up new leads and also impact a guilty conscience of a party involved in a serious criminal offense."

So far, that guilty party hasn't come forward.

33.
Who killed Russell Miller?
Janesville, 1996

Dawn Miller was awakened by her dog about 1 a.m. Dec. 3, 1996, then watched in terror as two black-clad figures raced up her basement stairs.

"I saw two people, men, run up the basement steps," she later told a jury. "I saw two people racing at me, coming up the steps dressed in black. My back was to the wall and I was crunched down. I guess I felt I would be safer than standing up. I was terrified."

She had reason to be scared. After the men left, she found her husband, Russell Miller, 33, severely beaten in the basement of their Janesville home. He died two days later at a local hospital.

Arrested for the murder were Joseph Bequette, 19, of Evansville, and Nathan Briarmoon, 22, of Janesville. They were charged with being parties to first-degree intentional homicide, robbery and burglary.

Prosecutors contended that Bequette and Briarmoon used a crowbar and hammer to beat Miller to death so they could rob him of hundreds of dollars in cash. The hammer and crowbar were recovered in a nearby creek.

Karen Odom, 16, of Janesville, also was charged with Miller's death and she testified that she and her friends played fantasy role-playing games with the victim such as Dungeons and Dragons. Odom testified she was in the car with Bequette and Briarmoon on the night they decided to kill Miller. Her testimony for the prosecution won her a deal to get her case disposed of in juvenile court.

"She thought he was a creepy old man," District Attorney David O'Leary said of Odom's attitude toward Miller. "He called her all the time. Gave her a pager so he could find her and threatened her friends if she didn't talk to him."

According to the criminal complaint, the girl and the two men "had been talking about doing something to Russell Miller for approximately three months, including making statements that they wished somebody would kill him."

The young people hated Miller so much they started a

"Get Russell Miller" club and pooled their loose change, according to trial testimony.

Before settling on Bequette and Briarmoon as the prime suspects, police investigated but discounted the possibility that Miller's wife set up her husband's murder because she stood to receive $350,000 in insurance money.

During closing arguments, defense attorneys attacked the credibility of Odom's testimony. They claimed she lied when she testified that Bequette and Briarmoon drove to a street near Miller's home, left her in the car for a while, returned and dumped something into a nearby creek. They said others had motives to kill Miller, including Odom's boyfriend.

Odom had testified she often lied to police officers because she was afraid of them. She also testified she first lied about the murder because she didn't want to get her friends in trouble, then decided to tell the truth.

But jurors didn't believe her. After 2 1/2 hours of deliberations, a Rock County jury found Bequette and Briarmoon innocent of the murder of Russell Miller.

After Bequette and Briarmoon were cleared of the murder, the Janesville Police Department closed the Russell Miller murder investigation.

"Following the verdict, we reviewed (the investigation) one more time," said Lt. Steve Kopp. "Investigators are prosecutors are satisfied we identified the right parties. The investigation is now closed."

That means no one will ever know for sure who beat Russell Miller to death. Was it Bequette and Briarmoon as police still believe? Or was it someone else as the jury ruled?

34.
Who killed Christine Rothschild?

Madison, 1968

On a Sunday night in May 1968, a student decided to peek in a window at the University of Wisconsin's Sterling Hall to see if a friend was working. Instead of his friend, the student found the body of Christine Rothschild in a clump of bushes.

Rothschild, 18, had been viciously stabbed at least a dozen times and strangled, possibly in broad daylight.

She was described as modest, studious and very attractive, wearing her hair long and straight in the style of the time. She had graduated with honors from Senn High School on Chicago's North Side, where she lived with her mother and three sisters. She had worked the previous summer as a fashion model at Chicago Loop department stores. Her father operated a brokerage firm and a company that sold coin-operated parking grates, which he invented in the 1950s.

Christine Rothschild planned to study journalism and enjoyed early morning walks. During her walk that Sunday morning, she had stopped for breakfast with a man.

The brutal murder shattered the innocence of Madison's campus community. Worse yet, police were unable to make an arrest despite a five thousand dollar reward.

A mental patient confessed to the murder, but detectives discounted the confession after looking at hospital records. Another man suspected of attacking three

Carthage College students in Kenosha also was ruled out.

The knife was believed to be a surgical-type blade and three investigators questioned a doctor in New York who had been on the UW-Madison campus at the time, but they couldn't prove his involvement. The knife never was found.

Two years later, detectives again traveled to the East Coast to question a graduate student who had worked in Sterling Hall at the time of the murder. But that lead, like the others, soon evaporated.

35.
Who killed Tanya Miller?
Milwaukee, 1986

Tanya Miller, 19, was found strangled Oct. 11, 1986. Her body was lying between a house and a garage in the 2100 block of North 28th Street. A "clove hitch" was used to tie her up.

Tanya Miller was one of the first of a dozen Milwaukee women killed over the next decade.

A Milwaukee man familiar with knot-tying was questioned in the deaths of some of the other women but police didn't have enough evidence to charge him with murder.

Another man, George L. "Mule" Jones, confessed to one of the murders and was implicated in several others in which the women had been strangled with the killer's bare hands instead of rope or clothesline.

36.
Who killed Marvin Collins and Ervin Schilling?

Friendship, 1974

When Marvin Collins and Ervin Schilling were found shot death in a small chainsaw shop run by Collins, detectives quickly zeroed in on a suspect.

Later that day, Dec. 11, 1974, police arrested Kenny Ray Reichhoff, a 19-year-old pulp cutter who worked for Collins and lived in a rented trailer next door.

The case against Reichhoff seemed strong. Prosecutors contended Reichhoff killed Collins to settle an argument four days earlier and that he

Kenny Ray Reichoff

shot Schilling, a customer, to silence him. They found Reichhoff's .22-caliber pistol, which they said was the murder weapon, hidden under Reichhoff's porch.

In July 1975, a Juneau County jury in Mauston convicted Reichhoff of two counts of murder and he was sentenced to two consecutive life prison terms. The trial was moved to Mauston from Adams County because of extensive pre-trial publicity.

The case appeared unremarkable and typical of hundreds of murders in which a dispute turns violent. And like many convicts, Reichhoff claimed he was innocent. He offered to take a lie detector test to prove it.

His family believed in him and offered a $1,000 reward for information leading to the arrest and conviction of the real killer of Collins and Schilling.

The Reichhoff family got *Wisconsin State Journal* reporter Richard Jaeger interested enough in the case's discrepancies to launch his own investigation.

The State Crime Laboratory found eight latent fingerprints in the chainsaw shop that didn't match Reichhoff or the victims. Prosecutors contended that Reichhoff entered the shop by a rear door when he killed the two men, but testimony showed the door had been barred and padlocked at the time.

Detectives also didn't consider that Collins' wife, who normally would have been at the shop, may have been the intended victim. Instead of opening the shop as usual that day, Mrs. Collins had gone to the hospital to pick up her son. Reichhoff probably didn't know that Mrs. Collins wasn't there and he had no dispute with her.

Experts also differed on whether the .22-caliber bullets that killed Collins and Schilling came from Reichhoff's .22-caliber Ruger automatic pistol. Police had confiscated another gun that belonged to Claude Hayes, Collins' father-in-law, but never tested it to see if it matched any of the spent shell casings.

"As far as I am concerned, Reichhoff was railroaded," said Vern Herrell, a former constable. "There was only circumstantial evidence introduced and none of it was enough to convict him.

Cracks in the case were enough to win a new trial for Kenny Ray Reichhoff and, in October 1977, a new jury overturned the murder conviction, setting Reichhoff free. The turning point was the failure by police to test the gun that belonged to Claude Hayes, who had died by the time of the new trial. In his second trial, Reichhoff was represented by flamboyant defense attorney Jack McManus. Attorney Richard Lent was appointed as a special prosecutor.

On Oct. 10, 1978, the body of Nancy Potts, 21, a licensed practical nurse, was found stuffed in the trunk of a car. The car had been bought as a mutual wedding gift for Potts planned to marry Reichhoff on Oct. 14. She had disappeared after leaving her job at Adams County Memorial Hospital.

Janna Lynn Henningsen, 22, the daughter of Adams County Sheriff Edwin Williams, was convicted of killing Potts. A witness said she saw Potts go into the Henningsen trailer on Oct. 10, but never saw her come out.

Henningsen was convicted by a Calumet County jury of beating Potts over the head with a frying pan and strangling her with a scarf after luring her into her trailer. A thirteen-year-old baby-sitter told police she saw the murder and was forced to help dispose of the body.

At the time of the 1974 murders, Henningsen had lived with Reichhoff's older brother and had testified on Reichhoff's behalf at his murder trial. A witness at her murder trial testified that Henningsen hated Potts and wanted to see her dead.

The Reichhoff case led to reform of Wisconsin's innocent convict compensation law. But by 1980, investigators said the murders of Collins and Schilling were too old to solve.

"We examined the trial transcripts, state crime lab records and law enforcement investigative files in the case and felt it would take more time than we could afford to spend to pursue it," said Frank Meyers, administrator of the state Division of Criminal Investigation, in 1980. "Our review of the evidence indicated it would take an admission by the person or persons involved in order to solve it."

In reality, many detectives still believed that Reichhoff was the killer despite the jury's verdict.

Did Kenny Ray Reichhoff murder Collins and Schilling that day? Or was it someone else?

37.

Who killed Officer Hans Lindstrom?

Elkhorn, 1927

When he made a traffic stop, Elkorn Officer Hans Lindstrom preferred preventative warnings to arrest. Perhaps that's what he intended when he stopped a Ford coupe about a mile northeast of Elkhorn on June 13, 1927.

Lindstrom, a Swedish immigrant and World War I veteran with four years of experience on the force, parked his motorcycle in front of the car after pulling it over. As Mrs. Frank Steinbicer watched from her sewing room window, the motorcycle cop and the car's driver got into an argument.

The car driver started backing up and Lindstrom moved his motorcycle to close to the right fender. The argument continued, and the driver backed up again.

"Suddenly I heard three shots in quick succession and then the car started coming this way," Mrs. Steinbicer told the *Elkhorn Independent*. "As the machine started, a fourth shot was fired and the car fairly flew past our house going north."

Lindstrom's body was found on the side of the road. One of his legs was under the motorcycle while the other was over the frame. He had been preparing to pursue the driver when the shots were fired.

Despite a $1,500 reward, the murderer never was found.

"If there is such a thing as the perfect crime, the murderer of Officer Lindstrom committed it," said the *Elkhorn Independent.* "He left practically nothing which could be used to bring him to justice."

38.
Who tried to burn down the mayor's house?
Madison, 1994

Paul Soglin, who served two stints as mayor of Madison, always was controversial. During his first stint in the 1970s, Soglin gained national prominence as the city's "hippie" mayor. Later, in the late 1980s and early 1990s, an older Soglin was less radical but still passionate about some of his political views.

In March 1994, Soglin's neighbors across the street were having a party. When two party-goers stepped out on the porch for some fresh air, they noticed a faint glow of flames from the Soglin's backyard.

"The Soglins must be having a bonfire," one said.

Paul Soglin

But it wasn't a bonfire. Someone had poured gasoline on the front and back steps of the Soglin home, lighted a torch and left it to burn. Soglin, recovering from heart bypass surgery, was inside with his wife, Sara, their three daughters and his mother, Rose.

The torch failed to ignite the blaze. Gasoline fumes awoke Rose Soglin, and the family found empty gas containers and the burned out torch lying in the snow.

Over the next three years, police compiled more than 200 pages of police reports on the incident, but failed to identify a suspect.

Police checked the possibility of an anti-Semitic motive and investigated whether right-wing extremists James and Theodore Oswald might have been involved. They also investigated threats made against Soglin during the 1970s.

They tried to find the origin of the gasoline containers, questioning people at two local restaurants, but still came up empty.

Soglin was convinced the most likely suspects were pro-gun activists angry about his gun control efforts. The mayor championed a gun control referendum.

It's unlikely the would-be arsonists and killers will ever be found.

39.

Who killed Terry Dolowy?

La Crosse, 1985

Terry Dolowy was a straight-A student at the University of Wisconsin-LaCrosse. She was athletic with a future in banking, and planned to marry her fiancé of five years.

But the 24-year-old woman's life was cut short on Feb.

14, 1985, after she returned to her trailer home about 1 a.m. from her job at Piggy's on Front Street, a tavern-restaurant.

Her headless and burned body was found four days later dumped in a roadside ditch along Mohawk Valley Road in northern Vernon County. Her pet poodle, Suzie, which Dolowy carried wherever she went was never found. The cause of death was undetermined.

Dolowy lived with Russell Lee, her boyfriend of five years, and they planned to marry after graduation in May that year. She was majoring in finance and planned to work in banking in the Chicago area where her father, Herbert Dolowy, was a banking executive.

During her senior year at River Forest High School in suburban Chicago, she had been named athlete of the year. She often was seen jogging along Highway M near the Boatwick Trailer Court at Barre Mils where she lived with Lee. The couple were vegetarians and often encouraged other family members to watch their health.

Dolowy also was an accomplished pool player and won the Association of College Unions International billboards tournament at La Crosse the month before her death.

When she got home from her job, Dolowy's boyfriend usually took the car and left for his job as a night auditor at the Radisson La Crosse Hotel..

"I think someone followed her home from her job at Piggy's, waited outside her trailer until her boyfriend left for his job and then called on her," said then-Vernon County Sheriff Geoffrey Banta. "That person then talked her out of the trailer and into a vehicle and kidnapped and killed her."

Banta believed the killer was someone she knew who was able to talk Dolowy into coming outside because there was no sign of a struggle. No blood was found where the body was dumped. One theory was that she was held captive for three days before she was killed.

A neighbor reported seeing Dolowy leave her trailer and get into a large, dark car with a short person early in the morning but wasn't sure if it was the morning she disappeared or a few days earlier.

Detectives questioned over a hundred friends and acquaintances of the popular college student and a reward fund was established, but the killer wasn't found.

A promising life was cut short that winter and someone so far has gotten away with a vicious murder.

40.

What happened to Catherine Sjoberg?

Concord, 1974

Seventeen-year-old Catherine Sjoberg, a senior at Oconomowoc High School, was attending her high school prom on the night of June 7, 1974, at the Concord Recreation Center in Jefferson County.

She had a disagreement with her date and walked out, leaving him standing. She was never seen again.

Her date that night was a prime suspect, but he passed three lie detector tests related to the incident.

Six years later, the Concord Recreation Center would be the scene of another crime. Kelly Drew and Tim Hack left a wedding reception there and both were murdered. That case also remains unsolved.

Detectives hoped for a break in the Sjoberg case in early 2000 when remains of an unidentified young woman were found in New Jersey. But a comparison of Catherine's dental records with the body showed no match.

Is Catherine still alive somewhere or was she brutally murdered? Was a vicious killer stalking events at the recreation center during the 1970s? Did someone who knew Catherine abduct her or was it a stranger?

41.

Who killed Deputy Walter Gaik?

Odanah, 1970

Deputy Walter Gaik of the Ashland County Sheriff's Department wasn't killed because he was a police officer. Gaik died because he happened to drive into the path of a man police described as a gun-crazy maniac killer.

The killer also was suspected in the shooting of an Ontonagon woman a few days earlier.

"We are looking for someone mentally unbalanced who we believe is responsible for both shootings," Sheriff Joe Croteau told the *Ashland Daily Press*. "It appears to us that the man who fired that shotgun that killed Deputy Gaik was not looking for Gaik, but was looking for someone to kill. The maniac killer set up a trap for whoever might move into it."

The man waited in the brush near a road that ran along the west bank of Bad River. The ambush site was at a large bridge a short distance south of Highway 2.

A few days earlier, Beatrice Fyfe, 54, of Ontonagon, was shot as she drove on Highway 2 into New Odanah, east of Bad River. Fyfe was injured by glass splinters in her legs and was treated at Ironwood Hospital, and survived. Gaik was killed after he was struck in the head by buckshot pellets from about ten to fifteen feet away.

The killer set up two tin cans in snow banks to mark the level of a driver's head when a car passed by. A shotgun was lined up with the cans, so it could be fired at a passing driver. The killer had dug a foxhole next to the village street to conceal himself.

When Gaik was hit, the pressure of his foot accelerated the car and it traveled northward more than two hundred feet before hitting a snowbank, spinning and coming to a stop.

Officers tracked the killer across the street and on to the ice of Bad River. The murderer then crossed the river, went up Highway 2 and crossed the bridge heading west.

Despite the assistance of the State Crime Lab, the killer could not be identified.

Gaik, a deputy for four years, previously worked for a railroad. He was the son of Ashland pioneer Stanley Gaik.

42.
Who killed Aloyzie Przybilla?
Trempealeau, 1997

When Leon Przybilla found his father's body on April 3, 1997, at his Trempealeau County home, authorities first thought the 74-year-old man had died of natural causes. But an autopsy determined he had been shot to death.

Pryzbilla's sons, Leon and Alan, have been relentless in the search for their father's killer. They mortgaged their homes to come up with $10,000 in reward money and spent $1,500 on telephone psychics to find information about their father's killer. They bought a chemical that detects blood and spread it around the room where the elder Pryzbilla was found.

"I can't help thinking that the last thing Dad was thinking when he went down was this: 'My boys aren't going to stop until they catch you,'" Leon Pryzbilla told the *La Crosse Tribune* in 1999.

Trempealeau County Sheriff's Lt. Dan Schreiner said some evidence in the case was destroyed because authorities assumed Pryzbilla died of natural causes until a pathologist at Sacred Heart Hospital in Eau Claire discovered he had been shot.

Schreiner said the elder Pryzbilla enjoyed weekend drinking parties and making illegal whiskey. He said he was called to the Pryzbilla farm several times to stop underage drinking parties. He said the victim's lifestyle could be connected to his murder.

"We have to consider a remote possibility that the events that occurred at the residence over the years may have contributed to this crime," Schreiner said in 1999.

Pryzbilla's sons said the parties eventually got out of hand and they helped stop them.

Did a disgruntled reveler or moonshine customer kill Aloyzie Pryzbilla? His sons have vowed they won't rest until they discover the truth.

"Dad had another ten or fifteen years left on him," Leon Pryzbilla said.

43.
Who killed Debra Bennett?
Madison, 1976

Debra Bennett was last seen walking barefoot along Loftsgordon Avenue in Madison, leaving an apartment from where she had been evicted. Her toes were painted and she wore blue jeans, carrying a denim

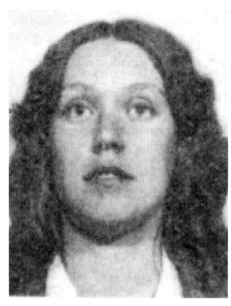

Debra Bennett

jacket and a brown shoulder-strap purse.

She had rented a room at the Cardinal Hotel, but never had the chance to move in. Her partially decomposed body was found by land surveyors in a ditch along Old Sauk Road in Dane County on July 21, 1976.

Dr. Billy Bauman, who conducted the autopsy, said the woman probably had been dead about ten days. She was identified through dental records and by a fractured collarbone.

A native of Ridgeway, in Iowa County, Debra Bennett had lived in Madison about seven months. She was unemployed and her body was found a few days before her twenty-first birthday. Her death may have contributed to the death of her father, William R. Bennett, who died from an illness a few days after the body was found. A joint funeral for the father and daughter was held in Dodgeville.

Three weeks after Debra Bennett's body was found, the key to her rented room at the Cardinal Hotel was mysteriously mailed to the hotel. But police had few leads to solve the murder.

44.

Who killed Joyce Ann Mims?

Milwaukee, 1997

Joyce Ann Mims, 41, was found strangled June 20, 1997, in a vacant home in the 2900 block of North 5th Street on Milwaukee's North Side, by workers renovating the building.

Mims was one of a dozen black Milwaukee women murdered over a decade. Most were involved in prostitution, but Mims had no criminal record.

George L. "Mule" Jones pleaded guilty to one murder and was a suspect but never charged in as many as nine others.

Mims had known Jones since they lived in Cleveland, Mississippi before coming to Milwaukee. She partied with Jones and his girlfriend, known as Sugar Baby.

Jones, an unemployed laborer with a ninth grade education, was convicted of stabbing a woman to death in Mississippi, and sentenced to five years in prison.

He apparently had difficulty performing sexually and allegedly killed Shameika Carter, 24, when she joked about his sexual inadequacy. Jones pleaded guilty to killing Carter.

During a lie detector test, an examiner determined that Jones was lying when he denied killing Mims. But he wasn't charged with her murder.

Police seized several items during a search of Jones' home including a black ski mask torn between the eyes and mouth, a red bra, a black high heel shoe and nine other women's shoes.

Besides Mims, Jones also was identified as a suspect in

the murders of Vernell Jeter in February 1990 and Mary Harris in September 1993.

45.
Who killed Mark Justl?

Madison, 1972

When Arthur Foeste of Madison delivered a news paper to the Joyce Funeral Home on on Nov. 22, 1972, he spotted a body at the end of a lighted front entrance hallway.

Foeste called police, who found Mark Justl, a funeral home worker, had been strangled. They found no evidence of forced entry.

An upstairs office and a basement storage room had been ransacked, but less than $10 was missing from an unlocked desk. Detectives believed that Justl may have interrupted a burglary, or one or more of the killers messed up the offices after the slaying.

Justl had a black eye, bruised mouth and a bleeding wound on the head from a fist or unknown object. He had fingernail scratches on his face and neck.

The night before, Justl had stayed until 1 a.m. at the 602 Club tavern on University Avenue. Then he had a hamburger and coffee at the Park Place Restaurant before heading home about 3 a.m. When his body was found, he was fully dressed, including a Navy pea coat and boots.

Justl lived at the funeral home and his roommate, Linford Smith, told police was sleeping in their ground-floor room at the rear of the funeral home. He had heard nothing.

A neighbor, however, said she heard scuffling sounds

and someone getting into a car about 3 a.m.

Mark Justl

When Justl was killed, he had one semester left for his law degree at UW-Madison Law School. But he had dropped out the year before to become coordinator of the Free University program.

Nearly 300 people were questioned in Justl's murder, but police failed to identify a suspect.

Less than six months after Justl's murder, his roommate, Linford Smith, was found dead of a self-inflicted gunshot wound in the woods on Picnic Point near Lake Mendota. Police found a .38-caliber pistol near the body.

Detective Charles Lulling said Smith, who then worked as a computer operator at Ray-O-Vac Inc., had passed four lie detector tests and was completely cleared of any involvement in the murder.

A year after the murder, Lulling said he remained hopeful that someone would be arrested for Justl's murder.

"This definitely is not a closed case," he said. "We're following new leads, even new information this week, but so far our investigations have resulted mostly in eliminating suspects rather than arresting them."

Who killed Mark Justl? Did his roommate commit suicide because he was involved in the murder? Or was Linford Smith distraught about Justl's death? The case remains unsolved.

46.

Who killed Barbara Nelson?

Edgerton, 1982

Barbara Nelson wasn't even supposed to work the night of Aug. 5, 1982, at the Mini Stop and Shop, a convenience store just off Interstate 90 near Edgerton. She got a call from Debbie Kortte, who owned the station, saying she needed Barbara to come in because an employee of another store owned by the Korttes had called in sick.

Barbara, 34, and her husband, Terry, were at home canning beans from their backyard garden. That fateful decision to go to work instead cost her life.

Barbara spent her early childhood on farms near Jefferson and Milton before her family moved to a subdivision east of Edgerton when she was a teenager. She had been an honor student at Edgerton High School and a church choir leader. She married Terry Nelson in June 1968, and a daughter, Rebecca Ann, was born 10 years later.

Barbara Nelson

Her husband was on voluntary layoff from a

job at Monterrey Mills in Janesville, and she had worked at the Mini Stop and Shop for about six weeks before her death.

When James Peterson pulled up to the pumps at the station about 5:40 p.m., Barbara appeared in the doorway of the convenience store and told Peterson they were out of gas. Peterson pulled away after he noticed a man with dirty, shoulder-length brown hair standing behind Barbara.

The next day, a teacher was driving home along a rural road east of Elkhorn when she saw a pickup truck parked along the roadside. She noticed a shorter person get pushed into the cab. Then a man got into the driver's seat and third person got into the back of the truck. The truck made a U-turn as the teacher approached, parking on her side of the road.

The teacher didn't want to get involved and didn't report the incident to police until after Barbara's body was found in a nearby cornfield four days later.

Detectives identified some suspects and still receive bits of information about the case once in a while, nearly two decades after the murder.

"It was really a tough case to work on because there wasn't a lot of solid information," Walworth County Sheriff Dean McKenzie told the *Janesville Gazette* in June 2000. "It was tough to get a motive. Why did they take her? Did they intend to release her? Did she do something out there, make a break for it? Why kidnap her at all? What's the motive? There was no demand for cash or ransom or anything."

McKenzie's questions and those of Barbara's family may never be answered, although a police official said during the summer of 2000 that detectives still worked the case and he expected they might be able to solve it.

47.
Who contributed to Dave Griswold's death?

Oshkosh, 1996

Dave Griswold of Appleton was driving on Highway 41 near Oshkosh on Sept. 7, 1996, when he was passed by a white Grand Prix driving recklessly at speeds estimated at 90 mph.

When the Grand Prix straddled the center line to pass between Griswold's pickup truck and another vehicle, Griswold sped up and caught the Grand Prix. The two drivers yelled obscenities at each other and exchanged obscene gestures.

The cars began swerving into each other and Griswold's truck lost control on the gravel shoulder, rolling into the ditch.

The Grand Prix sped away. Griswold, 37, died of massive head injuries a few days after the crash. Police searched without success for the driver of the Grand Prix.

Road rage killed Dave Griswold. According to the National Highway Traffic Safety Administration, road rage is the cause of a third of all fatal crashes, claiming 42,907 lives in 1996.

Cherilyn Eischen, a Winnebago County detective, said she doubted the other driver would ever be identified unless someone came forward.

"These two were playing cat and mouse down the highway," she said. "One guy lost his life and we have no idea who should be made accountable."

48.
Who killed the Weibel family?
La Crosse, 1992

When the bodies of Celia and Leroy Weibel, along with Celia's daughter Suzette, were found Sept. 27, 1992, in their mobile home southeast of La-Crosse, suspicion soon turned to James Frydenlund, who was Suzette's estranged husband.

The three had been beaten to death. Celia was 55, Leroy was 57 and Suzette was 29.

The Frydenlunds' two children, Jessica, 6, and Mathew, 2, were found unharmed in the mobile home at Brookview Mobile Home Park.

James Frydenlund, 35, of Minneapolis denied he had anything to do with the murders and claimed he was home alone that night. But he was arrested and jailed on $1 million cash bond more than a year after the triple slaying.

Prosecutors claimed Frydenlund drove from Minneapolis to La Crosse, killed the family and returned home before daylight. Suzette had complained about her marital problems in letters to her friends.

At Frydenlund's trial, defense attorney Earl Gray fingered Rocky Borck, Suzette's brother, as the killer. Gray accused detectives of planting hair evidence in the mobile home to implicate Frydenlund. Four of four hundred hairs examined from the crime scene were found to be consistent with samples of Frydenlund's hair.

Gray said Borck could have killed the family because he was upset with his mother for refusing to give him money to support his $200-a-month marijuana habit.

A jury deliberated over four hours before finding Frydenlund innocent.

"As far as we are concerned, there are no mystery suspects out there," District Attorney Scott Horne said after the verdict.

Did James Frydenlund get away with murder? Or was the killer someone else?

49.

Is there a Bray Road beast?

Elkhorn, 1991

Awoman was driving along Bray Road near Elkhorn when she thought she hit something. What could only be described as a terrifying beast leaped into the trunk, scraping its nails on the car and leaving claw marks before she managed to speed away..

The woman wasn't only person to have an encounter with what became known as the Bray Road beast. Others who claimed to have seen it described the animal as dog-like or wolf-like with brown fur. Some witnesses said it looked more like a bear.

But the most disturbing characteristic was that the beast was able to walk on its hind legs like a human. It was said to steal chickens and chase deer. It was said to have large fangs and glowing eyes.

Sgt. John Hawkinson of the Walworth County Sheriff's Department said in 1992 that he filed reports about the beast in a file marked "unfounded."

Linda Godfrey, a writer and cartoonist for a weekly newspaper in Walworth County, interviewed people who claimed to have seen the beast and wrote stories for the local paper as well as a national tabloid.

Only a few people believed the beast to be a were wolf but some entrepreneurs began selling werewolf hunting licenses. There is no record of anyone injured by the beast.

Mildred Bray, who lived on Bray Road, who lived on Bray Road with her husband, Dean, said she knew nothing about a beast and that her husband had lived there for nearly 80 years.

Another encounter was reported in 1999 in an account posted on the Weird Wisconsin web site (www.weird-wi.com). A witness said the beast didn't walk smoothly like a deer but bobbed up and down like a dog or wolf. She said it was at least five feet tall.

Is there a Bray Road beast or is the legend a product of overactive imaginations on moonlit nights in rural Wisconsin?

50.
Who killed Milwaukee police officers?

Milwaukee, 1917

When a bomb exploded at a Milwaukee precinct station on November 24, 1917, eleven people were killed in one of the worst tragedies in Wisconsin history. The dead included nine police officers and a woman who paused in front of the station just long enough to lose her life.

The bomb had been placed in an alley behind a church and brought to the precinct station for examination. When it exploded in a downstairs room, second-shift detectives had just completed their briefing upstairs.

One reason so many people died was that the police

weren't cautious enough in handling the dangerous device. After the fatal explosion, they sent for Sgt. Mike Mills, a bomb expert from the Chicago Police Department. Based on the deaths and devastation, Mills said the bomb was the most powerful he had ever seen.

But the police were not the original target of the bomb. The intended victim was the Rev. August Giuliani, pastor of the Italian Evangelical Church.

Giuliani was scheduled to be a key witness in the trial of several people involved in the Bay View riot on September 9, 1917. The minister, who had emigrated from Italy six years earlier, had broken with the Roman Catholic Church and encouraged immigrants to support the draft and serve in the Army during World War I.

On September 9, a group of anarchists showed up to disrupt a speech by Giuliani. Detective Albert Templin, later killed in the station explosion, began searching one of the gang members. Another gang member pulled a gun and shot and wounded Templin, unleashing a full-fledged riot.

Six suspects were rounded up two days after the station blast. Several rioters were convicted of intent to murder at a two-week trial. But no one was arrested for the station bombing.

51.

What happened to Woody Kelly?

Kenosha, 1985

Woodrow Scoval Francis Kelly Jr. left Kenosha Harbor on June 8, 1985, to try out a 42-foot fishing boat. When the boat was found several hours later in Lake Michigan near Zion, Illinois, Kelly had disappeared.

It seemed clear at first that Kelly somehow had been swept off the boat and drowned. But the debts and financial problems he left behind soon led investigators to the conclusion that he had faked his own death.

Kelly operated the Woodland Investment Co. in Gurnee, Illinois. When he disappeared, claims were beginning to mount against him in federal court by three hundred people in nine states who said he'd stolen the money they entrusted to him for investment. Over a four year period, Kelly had failed to account for $6 million.

About $75,000 of the $6 million was recovered in cash and jewelry from Kelly's estate.

Seven years after his disappearance, Kelly's former wife, Ann Proctor, filed a motion in court to declare Kelly dead so she could collect $250,000 from a life insurance policy. Insurance company lawyers fought the motion and won, persuading a Lake County, Illinois judge to rule against the motion in early 1994. Two people claimed they saw Kelly years after he supposedly drowned. The FBI stopped investigating the disappearance, assuming that Kelly was alive unless more evidence was found of his death.

Did Woody Kelly, an experienced yachtsman, drown in Lake Michigan that summer day? Or, did he fake his death to flee the hundreds of people he'd fleeced out of millions of dollars in his investment scams?

52.
Who killed William Paul?
Neenah, 1973

William Paul, one of Neenah's most popular businessmen, refused to give in to robbers on Aug. 6, 1973, and he died as a result.

Paul, 72, was found beaten in a pool of blood at his Midway Tavern. He never regained complete consciousness, and died sixteen days later.

One robber waited outside while two others entered and demanded money. One of the robbers threw a bar stool at Paul, knocking him down, then beat him with an undetermined object.

The robbers fled with $300 from the bar.

Fingerprints taken inside Paul's office and the bar were inconclusive. Two different types of blood were found at the scene. No murder weapon was found.

Hair samples also were taken from the scene and in 1991, investigators decided to compare a prison inmate's hair and blood samples with those found at the tavern.

53.

Who killed Officer T. Perry Gates?

La Crosse, 1900

When the La Crosse Police Department received word on September 8, 1900, that three desperadoes were headed their way, Officer T. Perry Gates had an idea how to stop them.

The men had beaten and robbed a La Crescent, Minnesota man in a boxcar.

Gates suggested that officers take a horse-pulled police wagon to the bridge over the Mississippi River and search the area. When Gates and another officer arrived at the bridge, they were told the men had come across about ten minutes earlier.

Gates found the three men at the corner of Third and King streets. He jumped out of the wagon, raised his gun and ordered the men to halt. The men lined up three abreast on the sidewalk and began firing at Gates.

"I did not see Perry fall," said Officer Schubert, who accompanied him to the scene. "The horse became frightened and went off like a cannon shot, in spite of my efforts to hold him."

As bullets whizzed by him, Schubert was unable to fire back or come to Gates' aid until he stopped the horse.

Gates died instantly and the entire La Crosse police force, along with some extra recruits, was sent out to scour the area for the killers. But they got away with murder.

54.
Who killed Derby Wagner-Richardson?

Racine, 1987

Derby Wagner-Richardson was in volved in a bitter divorce when she was kidnapped from her job as a security guard in the early morning of March 22, 1987.

Blood dripping from the drain holes in the trunk of her car led police to her body the next morning. Her throat was cut and her wrists had been slashed. She was gagged and naked.

Derby Wagner-Richardson

Wagner Richardson's estranged husband was viewed

as a suspect. But he maintained his innocence, and police never found enough evidence of his involvement to make an arrest.

The victim's mother, Ruth Wagner, took on finding her daughter's killer as a personal crusade.

"Some people would say I'm obsessed, but I don't agree with that," Wagner told a *Wisconsin State Journal* reporter in 1991. "Different things are therapy to different people."

Wagner also collected the letters she and her daughter wrote back and forth as a legacy for her two granddaughters that the murder left without a mother at ages four and seven.

The girls moved in with Wagner after their mother's murder. Wagner worked as a guard at Oakhill Correctional Institution near Madison.

55.
Where is Mark R. Meyer?
Sun Prairie, 1996

The last time anyone heard from Mark R. Meyer was on Dec. 7, 1996, when he talked on the phone to his daughter in Eau Claire, making plans for the holidays. Meyer, 45, a decorated Vietnam War veteran, also planned a hunting trip.

A few days after the call to his daughter, a neighbor walked in on one or more burglars searching Meyer's apartment on Park Circle in Sun Prairie. A second burglary was reported on Dec. 10, but Meyer could not be found. The burglars never were identified.

His 1978 Chevrolet Impala station wagon was found on Dec. 19 in the parking lot of a lumber supply store in Monona.

Sun Prairie Detective Bill Burton told a *Sun Prairie News* reporter that hundreds of people were interviewed and the burglaries were investigated, but no clue was found to Meyer's whereabouts. Police also checked bodies found as far away as Ohio to see if they might have been the missing man.

Meyer had run afoul of the law on drug possession charges. In May 1994, his arm was burned in a fire on Wilson Street in Madison.

"He was functioning pretty well in society," Burton said, and trying to turn his life around.

Mark R. Meyer

If Meyer had overdosed on drugs, committed suicide or died of a seizure, his body would have been found. He had a history of seizures and post-traumatic stress disorder.

"This is the first one that I know of that someone has just disappeared like this," Burton said. "Normally, they call eventually. Normally, there's some inkling that they're somewhere. This guy, he just dropped off the face of the earth."

56.
How did Tim Molnar die?
Waukesha, 1984

Tim Molnar, 19, told his mother he was going to aviation school when he left her Daytona Beach, Florida home in January 1984.

When his car, a 1969 Dodge Dart, was found in Atlanta a few months later, his mother began an intense search for her missing son. She distributed fliers, kept in touch with investigators and sought media attention.

In February 1996, the Molnar case was profiled on the television show "Unsolved Mysteries." A man watching the show in Waukesha County thought it might be related to a body he had found in the town of Merton in 1986.

The skeleton was found frozen in a sheet of ice in a pine forest. The only clue found with the body was a set of badly rusted keys.

Paul Konicek, Waukesha County deputy medical examiner, contacted Molnar's mother and asked if she still had the same locks on her house as when her son disappeared. She said yes and mailed Konicek a copy of her house key, which matched one of the keys found with the skeleton.

DNA tests later confirmed that the skeleton found in the sheet of ice was Tim Molnar.

But how did he die and why was his body found over a thousand miles from home? The skeleton showed no evidence of trauma and, although Molnar's mother said she found some peace in knowing the fate of her son, the circumstances surrounding his disappearance and death likely will remain a mystery.

57.
Why did Brian Littel die?
Waunakee, 1984

About 1:40 a.m. on the early summer morning of June 30, 1984, railroad engineer Timothy Deneen of Madison spotted something on the track in the flickering locomotive headlight.

As the train lumbered toward the object with a 6,000-ton load of gravel from the Rock Springs quarry, Deneen suddenly noticed the object looked like a man lying on the tracks. He applied the brakes and sounded the locomotive's blaring horn.

But Deneen couldn't stop the train in time. The engine struck the man before coming to a stop several hundred yards down the line. Brian Littel, 28, the victim, was rushed to the hospital where he was pronounced dead of severe head injuries.

Dane County Deputy Coroner Donald Scullion ruled Littel's death an accident. Littel was drunk and apparently fell asleep on the tracks. Authorities said they found no sign of foul play.

But Littel's mother, Patricia Hamm, wasn't so sure. She believed her son was murdered by members of the notorious Ghost Riders motorcycle gang who wanted to silence him about the murder a year earlier of Catherine Christian in a fatal fire near Stoughton.

Hamm said police failed to investigate Littel's death as a homicide.

"They didn't follow up on anything," she said six years later. "They didn't take any evidence. They didn't do an autopsy."

She believes her son was murdered by the Ghost Riders to cover up what he knew about the gang.

Brian "Punky" Littel was one of four children born to Patricia Hamm and her first husband, Gordon Littel, before they divorced in 1965. His mother said Brian Littel was nocturnal and didn't like to work much.

After he divorced Patricia Hamm, Gordon Littel married Geraldine Contreraz, sister of Ghost Riders outlaw Al "Big Al" Hegge, national president of the motorcycle gang.

The couple had three children before they also separated.

By 1982, Geraldine Contreraz was running Rosa's Cantina, a tavern near Stoughton. Because she was having trouble controlling her three teen-age children, she asked her by then ex-husband, Gordon Littel, to move into an apartment above the tavern. Littel agreed and moved in upstairs while Contreraz and the children lived downstairs.

Brian Littel also moved in with his father.

A new element had taken over the tavern, a group of bikers from the Northwest who called themselves the Ghost Riders. Hegge, their leader, was determined to start a chapter in the Madison area.

The gang's emergence on the local scene in 1982 became known quickly to police officers and motorcyclists. A Fitchburg home was bombed March 15, 1983, after several gang members were evicted.

A Jefferson County house occupied by members of a rival gang was burned two weeks later, and police believe members of the Ghost Riders could have set the fire.

In another incident, a man told police he was forced to perform a sexual act with a dog after a Ghost Riders gang member threatened him with a sword as part of an initiation rite into the gang.

On March 7, 1983, Catherine Christian, 22, died of smoke inhalation during a fire at Rosa's Cantina. Members of the Ghost Riders gang later were convicted of setting the fire and killing Christian.

A few weeks before the fatal blaze, Brian Littel had extinguished another fire at the rural tavern. Littel was in his upstairs apartment when he received a call from a sheriff's department dispatcher that a passerby had seen a fire in the tavern. Littel rushed downstairs and saw a wall of Contreraz's apartment ablaze. He put out the fire saving more than 100 pairs of shoes owned by Contreraz.

The night Christian died, Littel was out with this cousin, Doug McCartney. Afterward, Littel said he knew who had set the fire.

"They did it, Mom," he told Hamm. "I know the Ghost Riders did it. I heard them talking about it."

On the day he was killed by the train, Littel worked on a painting job with his brother. He was supposed to pitch that evening in a softball tournament, but the painting job went too late. His brother dropped off Brian at the Cosmo Club, a tavern where Doug McCartney was drinking.

McCartney suffered from pancreatitis but refused to give up his drinking as he awaited a transplant. About 8:45 p.m., McCartney got a call that a transplant pancreas had been found . He rushed to the hospital for the transplant, which extended his life for a couple of years but he eventually died of the same ailment.

After McCartney left, Littel went to the Willows Tavern in Waunakee, where he stayed until closing time. Eddie Glimme, the bartender, recalled that Littel was sober enough to help him fill the coolers after the bar closed.

Glimme asked Littel if he needed a ride, but Littel said he had one. When Glimme and the last customers left the bar, they saw Littel talking to a couple of guys near the horseshoe pits. A half hour later, Brian Littel was dead.

The train crew saw a car parked at a crossing near where Littel was struck, but police never identified the occupants.

Six months after Littel's death, arrest warrants were issued for ten members of the Ghost Riders gang and others for the murder of Cathy Christian. Four gang members, including Hegge, were found guilty of murder and drug possession in the state of Washington and were given life sentences. Two gang members accused of the Christian murder were never caught.

Patricia Hamm wrote to Dane County Sheriff Jerome Lacke, which prompted him to assign detectives to look into Littel's death.

Those detectives concluded that Littel's death was accidental. His blood alcohol level was 0.288 nearly an hour after his death, nearly three times the legal limit in Wisconsin for drunken driving.

They also found that Train No. 869E, which struck and killed Littel, was unscheduled, so there was no way the killers could have planned on the train coming through.

Detectives also interviewed Ghost Rider Ralph "Creeper" Jack, who said Littel was well-liked among gang members.

"Jack said Littel would not have been privy to any information about the gang's activities and little attention was paid to him," one police report said.

After the Jack interview, detectives closed the Littel investigation. Despite that conclusion, Patricia Hamm still didn't believe her son's death was an accident.

58.
Who killed Florence McCormick?

Milwaukee, 1995

Florence McCormick, 28, was found on April 24, 1995, tied up and strangled with a clothesline wrapped several times around her neck in the basement of a vacant house in the 600 block of Locust Street.

The cord was tightly knotted and tied to both wrists and the legs of a washtub. Her black lace bra was torn apart and she had red lace underwear stuffed in her mouth.

Workers who came to fix up the house discovered her body. She had been missing for two weeks and was one of a dozen women strangled in the same area during the decade. A "clove hitch" was used to tie her up.

A Milwaukee man familiar with knot-tying was questioned in the deaths of McCormick and some of the other women but police didn't have enough evidence to charge him with murder.

Another man, George L. "Mule" Jones, confessed to one of the murders and was implicated in several others in which the women had been strangled with the killer's bare hands instead of rope or clothesline.

59.
Who killed Julie Ann Hall?

Madison, 1978

On a summer day in 1978, a woman's body was found in a shallow grave along Woodland Road, just off Highway 12, west of Waunakee. She apparently had been killed by a blow from a blunt weapon. It took two days to identify the body as Julie Ann Hall.

Eighteen-year-old Julie Ann Hall grew up in Fennimore. On May 1, 1978, she got a job as a library assistant at the Wisconsin Historical Society on the University of Wisconsin-Madison campus.

She was the daughter of Donne and Betty Hall, who had won $300,000 three years earlier in the Illinois lottery. The couple divorced in 1977.

Julie had seven brothers, and one of them shared her apartment in the Park Village Apartments on Madison's

Julie Ann Hall

South Side.

She was last seen on a Friday night when she went out with friends. She was last seen drinking with a male friend at the Main-King Tap, east of Madison's Capitol Square.

In 1984, Madison and Dane County detectives went to a Texas prison to question Henry Lee Lucas, who had confessed to hundreds of murders while crisscrossing the nation with his partner, Ottis Toole. But Lucas suddenly had a change of heart and recanted his confessions, leaving the murder of Julie Ann Hall unsolved.

60.
Who killed James Elliott?

Beloit, 1989

James H. Elliott, 35, of Janesville, was found Jan. 7, 1989, slumped over the steering wheel of his pickup truck parked on a Beloit street, dead of a single bullet wound to his right temple.

Elliott's death might have been ruled a suicide. He was an avid deer hunter and owned a handgun for target practice.

"It was definitely not a suicide," said Julie Elliott, the victim's sister, told the *Beloit Daily News.* "That was the first thing I asked the police and they were emphatic it was not suicide. There was no gun in the truck, and my brother was not depressed or upset."

Police recovered a slug from inside the pickup truck. Elliott apparently had been shot at close range with a medium-caliber weapon. Elliott's deer-hunting rifle was found at his motel room, but the handgun was missing.

"We feel he took the gun down to Beloit to sell it for rent money," Julie Elliott said.

Perhaps James Elliott found a buyer for his handgun who decided he wanted it free and Elliott, instead of the would-be buyer, paid the ultimate price. The killer never was found.

61.

Who killed Officer Edward Riphon?

Madison, 1932

Ed Riphon allegedly had a "black book" that contained the names of known hoodlums, especially those in Madison's notorious Greenbush neighborhood.

Perhaps it was the information that Riphon collected about local gang leaders that got him killed on May 16, 1932. His beaten and bruised body was found in an abandoned gravel pit along Hope Road, east of Madison.

Riphon, 36, was killed by two bullets fired at close range. One struck him in the left part of his chest just below the heart. The other hit him in the left temple, penetrating his brain and coming out the back of his head.

His car was found parked at the State Capitol. His last report was shortly after 1 a.m. from a call box at Main and Pinckney streets on the Capitol Square. But a tipster told police he saw Riphon in a nearby restaurant about that time. While Riphon was in the restaurant, the tipster said he saw three men walking back and forth in front of the restaurant, peering inside the front window.

Patrolman Howard Collard reported that two men in a DeSoto roadster had stopped him on his beat shortly before midnight and asked were Officer Riphon could be found.

Riphon wasn't on his regular beat. His regular beat was along Baldwin Street on Madison's East Side, but he was assigned to patrol the Capitol area that night.

He apparently knew some of the gangsters in his book were after him. He seemed nervous to fellow officers.

Detectives considered the possibility that Riphon was killed when he interrupted a crime. But his "black book," and the other clues, made it more likely that he was stalked and murdered by one or more of the local gang leaders he profiled.

62.
Who killed Marilyn McIntyre?
Columbus, 1980

While her three-month-old son slept in another room, Marilyn McIntyre, 18, was beaten beyond recognition with a blunt object in her home on Ludington Street in Columbus on March 11, 1980.

Her husband, Lane, found her on the living room floor when he arrived home from work about 7 a.m. from his job at a paper mill. A green armchair was covered with blood. There was no sign of a struggle and the only furniture police found out of place was an overturned foot stool. Residents of a second-floor apartment above where McIntyre lived said they heard nothing unusual that night.

Robert Jones, a retired Columbus police officer who investigated the case, said there was a short list of suspects and some crime scene evidence, but no murder weapon was found. The coroner's report listed the cause of death as massive head injuries. She also was stabbed repeatedly.

Marilyn McIntyre

"It could have been one of those square glass ashtrays," he said. "We did find a baseball bat under a wood pile in the country but couldn't tell anything from it."

Police believe McIntyre knew her assailant because otherwise she wouldn't have opened the door and let him inside. She had a habit of keeping the door locked and not opening it until she had checked who was outside.

Nearly two years after the murder, the house where McIntyre was killed was damaged in a fire and torn down.

McIntyre's twin sister, Carolyn Rahn, refused to give up hope that the killer someday will be found.

"They say time heals all pain, not with something like this," she said in 1998. "He not only murdered her, he murdered the person I used to be. He has taken away my freedom and my trust in other people."

63.

Who killed Michael Fisher?

Superior, 1966

As usual, that morning in 1966, Michael Fisher, 14, brought up his wagon from the basement of his Superior home so he could fill it with newspapers for his paper route.

But Michael just delivered one copy of the *Superior Evening Telegram* that day and his wagon with two newspaper bundles was found by his sister, Valerie, 15, abandoned along Ogden Avenue. Valerie finished her brother's route, wondering what had happened to him.

The mystery of Michael's disappearance was cleared up about 9 p.m. that night, about twelve hours after Valerie Fisher had discovered her brother's wagon. Richard Vendela and Richard Orlowski were walking along Hill Avenue, about two miles away from the Fisher home, when they spotted something in the ditch. The had discovered Michael's body.

His head was wrapped in a red sweatshirt. He was lying on his back, fully clothed. There was no sign he had been molested and no bruises on his body to indicate there had been a struggle. Dr. Edward G. Stock, the Douglas County coroner, said the boy had been struck in the head by a single, crushing blow. He had died about fourteen to sixteen hours before the body was discovered, and apparently was dead before the body was dumped in the ditch.

Small puncture wounds found in Michael's head and neck led to early speculation he had been shot, but this later proved untrue. No blood stains were discovered where his wagon had been found.

"Was it an accident or was it done on purpose?" wondered Police Chief Charles Barnard. He said perhaps Michael was hit by a car and the panicked driver dumped his body. Or perhaps someone murdered the boy. But why?

Earlier that month, Michael had finished eighth grade at the Cathedral School and was looking forward to starting high school that fall. Besides his sister, he also had two younger brothers, Carl and Timothy. He was an altar boy at Cathedral Christ the King Church.

Within a day or two after the body was found, police began to rule out an accident as a probable cause of Michael's death. A car accident, especially one that killed a pedestrian, would have left some evidence – shattered glass, tire marks. But no sign of an accident was found on Ogden Avenue anywhere near where the wagon had been discovered. Even more ominous was the fact that a single item was missing – the wire cutters used by Michael to cut the steel tape around his newspaper bundles. Could the pair of wire cutters have been as the murder weapon?

Two days after Michael's death, the Superior Jaycees put up two hundred fifty dollars as the first contribution to a reward fund for information leading to the arrest and conviction of the boy's killer. The *Evening Telegram* upped the ante, pledging another two hundred fifty dollars. The City Council chipped in a hundred dollars.

Now that the police had ruled out an accident, catching Michael's killer turned into a community crusade. To nearly everyone in the lakeside city, it was a shocking crime, largely because an innocent victim was killed apparently without cause. It could have been anyone.

The State Crime Lab was called in to examine Michael's clothing. A hundred members of the local Civil Defense unit planned a shoulder-to-shoulder search of an area one hundred fifty feet on each side of Hill Avenue. They hoped to find the wire cutters, perhaps a fingerprint or another clue that would lead to Michael's killer.

The reward fund swelled to three thousand dollars. Police conducted a door-to-door canvass of the area along Michael's paper route. Greg Austreng discovered a pair of tin snips in a burning trash barrel along First Street. The cutters were examined by the Crime Lab. They were similar to the pair used by Michael, but no one could make a positive identification.

As the reward fund surpassed four thousand dollars, police finally had a break in the case. A witness said he saw Michael taken away that Sunday morning in a 1959 Chevrolet Biscayne with two men inside. The man went out on his porch to get the paper when he saw two men take Michael by the shoulder and put him in the front seat of the car. At the time, the witness said he thought one of the men probably was the boy's dad.

One man was described as about five feet six inches tall with a slender build, dark hair and a tan complexion. He wore blue jeans and a jean jacket. The other man stayed in the car and the witness said he didn't get a good look at him. The car was described as a two-tone, white or cream on top and orange or red on the bottom. It was polished to a bright sheen, the witness told police. He had been out of town, he said, and that's why he hadn't come forward earlier.

A three-state alert was issued for the car in Wisconsin, Minnesota and upper Michigan. Police in Minocqua arrested a middle-aged man on a traffic charge. He was from Superior and was in that city on the day of Michael's murder. Police also found blood on the front seat of his car.

Superior detectives rushed across the state to Minocqua. But the car didn't match the witness's description and the man later was released. In Superior, twenty-one cars did match the description but no evidence was found.

More than three decades after the brutal murder of Michael Fisher, the case remains unsolved. Was it a thrill killing by a pair of low-lifes out on a drunken binge? Did Michael somehow cross someone who decided to get even? Was robbery or sexual molestation a motive that somehow was thwarted? Did the killers strike again, and were they ever brought to justice for another crime?

It's likely these questions about Michael's brutal murder will remain unanswered.

64.
Who killed Debra L. Harris?
Milwaukee, 1986

Debra L. Harris, 31, was the first in a series of a dozen women killed on Milwaukee's North Side over the next decade. Her body was pulled from the Menomonie River, about 100 feet east of the Ember Lane Bridge, on Oct. 10, 1986. A "clove hitch" was used to tie her up.

A Milwaukee man familiar with knot-tying was questioned in the deaths of some of the other women but police didn't have enough evidence to charge him with murder.

Another man, George L. "Mule" Jones, confessed to one of the murders and was implicated in several others in which the women had been strangled with the killer's bare hands instead of rope or clothesline.

65.

Who killed
Dr. Thomas Andrew Speer?

Madison, 1971

Dr. Thomas Andrew Speer was a physician from Merrillville, Indiana, who came to Madison in July 1971 for a medical conference. He was shot to death shortly after 10 p.m. outside a motel on the city's southeast side.

Speer, who left a wife and three children, was killed in a drive-by shooting, years before such shootings plagued larger cities.

Witnesses said a blond or light-haired white man, about 30 to 40 years old, fired three shots at Speer as he walked toward the motel door. The gunman, who shot Speer from a car, then sped away in a yellow or gold, two-door, hardtop Chevrolet, possibly a 1968 or 1969 model with mud flaps.

Two of the three shots fired hit Speer, one in his left wrist and the other in his back. The second shot also hit his heart.

Paul Rand, who was vacationing in Madison and staying at the motel, witnessed the shooting. He said the man in the car said

Dr. Thomas Andrew Speer

nothing to Speer before firing the fatal shots.

Police searched the area around the motel with metal detectors in hopes of finding the gun used to kill Speer. An autopsy revealed he had been shot with a .22-caliber handgun.

Speer was on the North Western Railroad medical staff and a railroad detective described him as "too nice a guy to have any enemies in this world."

Two suspects were questioned in Speer's murder, but they weren't arrested.

66.
Who killed Connie Reyes?
Kenosha, 1990

Concepcion "Connie" Reyes, a Kenosha County social worker, left work about 11:45 a.m. on the Thursday before Easter in 1990, saying she wasn't feeling well.

It was the last time Reyes, 57, was seen alive. She probably drove home, parked her car in the garage and went into the house through the back door. She never got her mail, which was delivered about 12:45 p.m., or her evening newspapers.

Her partially nude body was found two days later by a close friend, JoAnn Slater, and Slater's husband.

Reyes had no known enemies, and police believe the killer was someone she knew and let in through the front door. Police found no evidence of robbery or forced entry.

Detectives interviewed her clients and coworkers and failed to develop any leads. Reyes also apparently wasn't involved with any nationalist groups in the Philippines.

She had relatives in her homeland and on the East Coast.

Seven detectives worked the case for a while but, two years later, only a couple of detectives still were assigned to it.

"Connie really believed in the system," JoAnn Slater said. "I hope it works for her. I wish they could find out who did it and that person would be brought to justice."

67.
Who killed little Annie Lemberger?

Madison, 1911

The kidnapping and murder of little Annie Lemberger on Sept. 6, 1911, is one of Wisconsin's most intriguing and longest-running murder mysteries.

Annie, who was just starting the second-grade, lived in a small frame house in the old Madison Italian neighborhood of Greenbush. She slept in a tiny, eight-foot-square bedroom with her sister and two brothers.

Sometime during the night of Sept. 5-6, little Annie vanished. Her mother had put the children to bed about 7 p.m. and the girl was gone by the next morning. The other children told authorities they hadn't heard a thing. Mrs. Lemberger said she'd locked all the doors and windows, including the one above Annie's bed.

The disappearance aroused outrage among many city residents. A crowd gathered outside the Lemberger home. Annie's father showed police officers how someone must have torn the mosquito netting on the outside, then removed a piece of cracked glass from the window above Annie's bed and reached inside to open it. Then, the culprit must have propped up the window with a piece of lath and quietly grabbed Annie from her bed and through the window.

Police found footprints under the window but they were ruined as evidence by the crowd stomping around outside. A band of gypsies was in town, and police searched their camp south of the city for the missing girl. Searchers combed vacant buildings, boxcars and storm sewers, but found no sign of her.

Newspapers raised questions about the case. What was the motive? Annie's parents were too poor to pay a ransom. Was she snatched by a child molester? If that was the case, then why would he risk breaking into the house when he could more easily grab Annie or another girl on the street? How could Annie be awakened by a stranger without screaming, especially when police found no evidence that an anesthetic had been used to subdue her? Why did Lemberger and his wife report hearing nothing, when the door to the room where they slept was ajar that night? And why was their noisy dog silent, keeping the intruder's secret?

Spurred by a two hundred dollar reward offered by the mayor for the girl's recovery, bystanders talked of a house-to-house search. Thousands of callers clogged phone lines at newspaper offices and police headquarters, seeking the latest word on whether the girl had been found.

On Saturday, George Younger, a cement worker, spotted something floating in Brittingham Bay and stopped at Bruno Kleinheinz's saloon for help to bring it to shore. It was the nude body of little Annie Lemberger.

An autopsy found no water in the girl's lungs, indicating she had been strangled or suffocated before she was dumped in the water. Bruises were found behind her left ear and over her left eye. Smaller bruises were found on other parts of her head.

Determined to get a leg up on its competition, the *Wisconsin State Journal* raised ten thousand dollars to hire crack investigator Edward L. Boyer of the William Burns Detective Agency in Chicago to assist police on the case.

On Sunday, more than four thousand people, nearly a fifth of Madison's entire population of about twenty-one thousand, showed up for a wake at the Lemberger home to get a look at the dead girl. Police had to limit the crowd to ten people in the tiny house at a time.

Early in the investigation, police began to suspect that John A. "Dogskin" Johnson could be the killer. Johnson, who lived down the block from the Lembergers, helped the family search for Annie on the day of her disappearance. But Johnson also had a criminal record. He had once damaged a train and assaulted three young girls. He was questioned about Annie's disappearance, then released. But on the day Annie's body was found, Johnson was taken into custody again.

Johnson had an alibi provided by his wife, Bertha, and their two daughters, Selma, age fourteen, and Bertha, age sixteen. The girls worked as strippers at the American Cigar Co. and said they'd been home that night when their father came home about 9 p.m.

By the following Tuesday, Boyer said he was at work on a new lead. Johnson seemed an unlikely suspect, although he remained in jail.

Questioning of Johnson continued and soon zeroed in on the girl's missing nightgown. At one point, a detective asked the suspect: "Where is the nightgown?" "I can't tell," Johnson replied. From that answer, the detectives concluded Johnson knew where it was but wouldn't tell.

Boyer also questioned Johnson, warning him to stay away from the window, where an angry mob had gathered outside, ready to lynch him.

On September 13, Johnson summoned turnkey John Foye and confessed to the murder. The same day, he pleaded guilty and was sentenced by Judge Anthony Donovan to life in prison. When he reached Waupun State Prison, Johnson breathed a sigh of relief. "Well, the mob didn't get me," he said. "And I didn't murder Annie Lemberger."

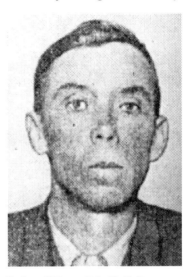

John "Dogskin" Johnson

Johnson had twice been admitted to Mendota Mental Health Institute, once for assaulting a young girl and the other time for attempted sexual assault of two girls, ages seven and ten.

After he arrived at Waupun, Johnson immediately began a campaign to prove his innocence of the Lemberger murder. Finally, in the fall of 1921, Gov. John J. Blaine agreed to hear Johnson's case.

Although a decade had passed since the murder, the case still hadn't lost its public fascination. More than a thousand people jammed the Senate chamber in the Capitol to watch the pardon hearing.

Johnson testified that his fear of the mob caused him to confess to a murder he didn't commit. But his testimony was refuted by several former police officers, who denied anyone coerced him into confessing to the crime. As the hearing recessed for the weekend, things were not going well for Johnson.

When the hearing resumed on October 5 for closing arguments, Johnson's new attorney, Ole A. Stolen, had received permission to introduce new evidence.

"Now I am prepared to prove who killed Annie Lemberger," he told a hushed crowd. "Annie Lemberger came to her death by blows struck by her own father! Sheriff, serve your warrants."

Little Annie's father was arrested for second-degree murder. His wife and their son, Alois, were arrested for perjury.

Then Stolen called May Sorenson, a cleaning woman, to the witness stand. Sorenson testified that she was a friend of the Lemberger family who went to the home to provide comfort after the girl's disappearance. As she held nine-year-old Alois on her lap, Sorenson said Alois told her their father, angry that little Annie had been too slow to hand him a stove poker, had hit her on the head with a beer bottle. The father carried her to bed, but she died a few minutes later.

Sorenson claimed the boy told her the Lembergers paid $35 to a man named Davis to throw the girl's body in the lake. She also testified she found the blood-stained nightgown and tried to put it in the tub with the sheets from the girl's bed, but Mrs. Lemberger snatched it from her and threw it into the stove.

Johnson was freed and Martin Lemberger was charged with fourth-degree manslaughter, a crime for which the statute of limitations had expired four years earlier. He never went to trial.

But that wasn't the end of the sensational case. In 1933, the *Chicago Daily Times* hired Professor Leonarde Keeler of Northwestern University to administer lie detector tests to the Lembergers, Johnson and Sorenson. The lie detector was a new device and the newspaper wanted a case on which it could be tested.

The accuracy of the tests is debatable. The Lembergers passed when they denied that Martin Lemberger killed his daughter. Johnson was nervous throughout the tests, but his nervousness may have been just a personality trait. But when Sorenson failed the test, she admitted that she was offered five hundred dollars to lie in her testimony against Lemberger.

The recantation destroyed the key evidence against Lemberger, but failed to shed any light on the mystery of Annie's death. Did Annie's father kill his daughter in a drunken rage as May Sorenson alleged? Or was Dogskin Johnson the culprit, as police first believed?

68.
Why did Lorelei Jane Bringe die?
Poynette, 1988

The first thing Stan Banach noticed when he arrived at his daughter's Poynette home on Aug. 19, 1988, was his son-in-law, Mark Bringe, leaving in a hurry. Banach went upstairs and began unpacking his bags in the bedroom where he usually stayed.

When Bringe got home, Banach asked where his daughter was. When Bringe called out for her and didn't get an answer, the two men went outside to look for her. Banach found his daughter lying along a path.

"I said, 'Oh, my God,' as I saw blood coming from her mouth," Banach later said. "I saw a gun near her and thought, 'oh, no, she shot herself in the mouth.' I shouted for Mark to get some help and knelt down to hold her head."

Lorelei Jane Binge, who was known as Lori, was found shot to death with a single bullet to the left temple area of her head. Her husband, Mark, 42, worked as a Sun Prairie woodcrafter. He said Lori, 33, committed suicide over a love affair gone bad with a Detroit man or because she was depressed over a car accident.

Two .25-caliber, semiautomatic pistols were found on the right side of Lori's body along with an ammunition magazine loaded with four cartridges, and a leather holster. One gun had fired the fatal shot, but no shell casing was found. Lori was right-handed, but she was shot on the left side of her head.

Since Lori's death was assumed to be a suicide, the crime scene wasn't cordoned off to protect it and the State Crime Lab wasn't called in. Tests of Lori's hands to determine if she had fired the gun were botched.

When she was found, Lori wore the same dark blue business suit she had worn to work that day. She wore no shoes.

Lori's corpse was taken directly to a Portage funeral home where it was washed, embalmed and prepared for burial.

But Lori's other relatives didn't believe it was suicide. Her sister, Betty Talidis of Union, Illinois, hired a private detective to try to solve the case.

Mark Bringe planned to cremate his wife's body, saying she had requested it. But other relatives protested and authorities stopped the cremation until the case could be investigated.

Bringe said he picked up his wife at work early that day because her father was coming to visit.

"She was her usual quiet self and really didn't say too

much, or nothing I can recall," he said. "We stopped at the liquor store to get some more whiskey and some beer for her dad."

He said they arrived home about 4:30 p.m. and his wife got upset because the kids had messed up the playroom. Bringe said his wife told him she had books due at the library and he rushed out to return them.

Before leaving for the library, Bringe said he heard a gunshot, but thought it came from a firing range down the road. Others said they recalled hearing the shot later.

Bringe denied killing his wife and said he would take a lie detector test if it were administered by an independent examiner.

After the funeral, an autopsy ordered by the court was performed by Dr. Robert Huntington.

"Ordinarily this would be thought a suicide," Huntington wrote in his autopsy report. "Judgment as to manner should be done with care. Given the entry on the wrong side of head, with atypical long angle of entry and a lack of obvious powder in wound, homicide should be carefully ruled out."

A neighbor, Portage attorney Donald Plier, told the *Wisconsin State Journal* he couldn't believe that Lori would kill herself.

"I didn't think of it until later, but her body was in a strange position, on her back, but with blood running down her face from the wound, or uphill, more or less," he said. "I went back the next day and looked and couldn't see any blood on the ground. Boy, it sure didn't look like suicide to me."

Bringe said his wife made a lot of strange long-distance phone calls all over the country, but he had no idea who might want to kill his wife.

69.

Who killed Julie Speerschneider?

Madison, 1979

Sixteen-year-old Charles Byrd of Stoughton was hiking along the Yahara River on a Saturday afternoon in April 1981, when he came across a barely visible skeleton in an out-of-the-way clearing.

The body was identified as twenty-year-old Julie Speerschneider, who had disappeared two years earlier.

Julie Speerschneider left the 602 Club, a bar at 602 University Avenue, on the night of March 27, 1979, to go to a friend's house. She was wearing blue jeans, boots and a blue-and-gray striped Mexican poncho when she and a male companion hitchhiked along Johnson Street.

Julie Speerschneider

The driver of a compact, white four-door car had picked up the pair on State Street and left them off at Johnson and Brearly streets. Her hitchhiking companion never was identified.

At the time of her disappearance, Julie worked at the Red Caboose Day Care Center and at Tony's Chop Suey Restaurant.

Friends and relatives circulated her photograph, offered a $500 reward and consulted a psychic to locate her.

Detectives who questioned Henry Lee Lucas in 1984 at a Texas prison believe he and sidekick Ottis Toole may have killed Julie Speereschneider. Lucas, who confessed to hundreds of murders across the country, passed through Wisconsin in his way to visit relatives in Minnesota. But Lucas later recanted his confessions.

70.
Why did Susan McFadden die?
Wisconsin Dells, 1990

It wasn't hard to figure out how Susan McFadden, 23, of Baraboo, died in March 1990. She fell 45 feet to her death from a tall pine tree at Mirror Lake State Park.

But why was McFadden, a student at Madison Area Technical College, climbing the tree in the middle of the night?

She was found face down about six feet from the base of the tree, after her family initiated a search for her. Her mother reported her missing when she failed to return home.

Her socks and shoes were found nearby. Her blouse, which she apparently removed before starting the climb, was found near the body, along with a pack of cigarettes, butane lighter, plaid jacket and car keys.

When forestry experts cut down the 52-foot tree, they found a missing bough that matched a broken one found near the body. Other broken branches were found at various levels that marked the course of her fall.

"They feel this is the one she reached up to make the pull to pull herself one step higher, and the branch broke," said Sauk County Sheriff Virgil Steinhorst.

No indication was found that McFadden had been drinking alcohol, but toxicology tests found traces of cocaine and marijuana in her blood.

Police questioned and cleared a former boyfriend who had been placed under a restraining order the previous year for threatening her.

Was Susan McFadden on a drug-induced high when she made the fatal decision to climb to the top of that pine tree? Or was she running from something or someone?

71.

Was Lawrencia Bembenek guilty of murder?

The Lawrencia Bembenek case may have been Wisconsin's most intriguing mystery of the 1980s, spawning several books and made-for-television movies. Bembenek, whose nickname was "Bambi," was an attractive former Milwaukee police officer and former Playboy Club waitress.

On May 28, 1981, someone broke into the home of Christine Schultz, fatally shooting her and attempting to strangle her son, Sean. A scarf was wrapped around Christine Schultz' neck.

The victim's ex-husband, Elfred Schultz, was on duty as a Milwaukee police officer. He rushed to her house to comfort his two terrified sons.

The killer was described as someone with a red ponytail and wearing a green Army fatigue jacket. A neighbor told detectives someone had broken into his garage on the night of the murder and stolen a green jogging suit and a .38-caliber revolver.

Bembenek said she was asleep when she got a call about 3 a.m. from her husband, Elfred Schultz, who said his ex-wife had been murdered. An hour later, detectives rang Bembenek's doorbell. They asked if she owned a gun or green jogging suit. She said no and they left.

Bembenek became a suspect due to a bitter dispute between Elfred and Christine Schultz over alimony. Killing Christine Schultz was a violent way to resolve it, which gave Bembenek a motive.

Judy Zess, a former roommate of Bembenek's, came forward and told investigators she had heard Bembenek threaten to kill Christine Schultz. Zess claimed that Bembenek was angry about the amount of alimony demanded by the ex-wife, and that Bembenek was jealous of her husband's first wife.

The case was circumstantial until a reddish brown wig was discovered in the plumbing of the building where Bembenek and Elfred Schultz shared an apartment. Nearly a month after Christine Schultz was killed, Bembenek was arrested for murder.

Detectives believed Bembenek put on a green jogging suit, grabbed her husband's off-duty revolver and jogged to Christine Schultz' home about two miles away. After trying to strangle Sean and killing his mother, she jogged back home.

Bembenek hired Donald Eisenberg, a flashy Madison attorney who enjoyed notoriety and high-profile cases. He asked for a $25,000 retainer and promised her the charges would be dismissed at the preliminary hearing.

But the charges wouldn't go away that easily. Judy Zess testified that Bembenek once told her she would pay to have Christine Schultz "blown away." And Bembenek's husband was granted immunity from prosecution in exchange for his testimony against her.

It wasn't the first time Judy Zess had testified against Bembenek. In August 1980, Bembenek was among three women police officers fired by Police Chief Harold Brier. Zess had signed a statement accusing Bembenek of smoking marijuana at a concert.

Out of work, Bembenek took a job as a waitress at the Lake Geneva Playboy Club. She later worked as a

Marquette University security guard. But she battled to get her Milwaukee police job back. She came across some nude photos of Milwaukee police officers taken at a picnic and showed them to one of her friends on the force. She also began dating Elfred Schultz, one of the officers in the photos.

Although the evidence mounted against her, Sean Schultz insisted that the person who tried to strangle him was a man wearing an Army

Lawrencia Bembenek

fatigue jacket, not a green jogging suit.

At her trial, Bembenek testified for five hours, providing details about how she met Elfred Schultz, the nature of their relationship and her actions on the night of the murder. She also testified about harassment from the Milwaukee Police Department and the fight to win her job back.

But Bembenek's testimony was rebutted by two powerful prosecution witnesses. Marilyn Gehrt testified that she had sold Bembenek a wig a year earlier. Annette Wilson, a security guard at the Boston Store, testified that Bembenek once stole a green jogging suit from the store.

On March 9, 1982, after several days of deliberations, the jury found Bembenek guilty of first-degree murder. A year later, an appeals court upheld the conviction.

The verdict only heightened the debate over whether Bembenek was guilty. Some people believed she was a black widow spider, beautiful but deadly. Others couldn't believe such an attractive women would commit such a horrible crime.

Ira Robins, a Milwaukee investigator, began a one-man crusade to free Bembenek. He was a former Milwaukee police officer who suffered discrimination over his Jewish heritage. Robins became Bembenek's man on the outside, using his detective skills to follow up her leads and try to find another suspect.

Another Bembenek admirer, Jacob Wissler, devised a hit-man theory to get close to her. He offered $20,000 to Joey Hecht, convicted of the 1983 murder of Carolyn Hudson in Madison, if Hecht would confess to killing Christine Schultz. In prison, Hecht bragged that the Hudson murder wasn't his only contract killing. Wissler also offered $25,000 to Michael Durfee, Elfred Schultz' partner, to retract his testimony. Wissler also wrote a series of love letters to Bembenek.

Martin Kohler, Bembenek's latest attorney, filed a motion for a new trial in 1987, based on the investigation by Robins. Judge Michael Skierawski denied the motion in November 1988.

Nick Gugliatto was visiting his sister at Taycheedah state prison when Bembenek first saw him. Soon afterward, they began writing letters back and forth. On July 15, 1990, less than a month after an appeals court denied Bembenek's motion for a new trial, she climbed over the prison fence and fled with Gugliatto to Canada.

The escape rekindled the public's fascination with the case. In Milwaukee, Robins tried to capitalize on the renewed interest, organizing a rally and enlisting public support for a new trial. Bembenek's picture was splashed across television screens until, finally, in October, a tip to the program "America's Most Wanted" led police to her in Thunder Bay, Ontario, where she was working as a waitress under the name of Jennifer Lee Gazzana.

Bembenek's fight against extradition piqued the interest of Canadian authorities. Her dramatic escape and capture generated more than a little interest from U.S. authors and moviemakers. In the bright eye of publicity, Bembenek seemed to forget her romantic promises to Gugliatto, who was sentenced to a year in the Fond du Lac County Jail for his role in the escape. Mary Woeherer, Bembenek's new attorney, filed a motion for a secret John Doe investigation into the case. It was granted by Judge William Haese.

On November 30, 1991, Frederick Horenberger shot and killed himself after committing an armed robbery. Horenberger had evolved as Robins' prime suspect in the Christine Schultz murder. Just before he died, Horenberger denied killing Schultz. But Robins couldn't give up the notion that easily. He reasoned that Horenberger committed suicide rather than become the target of the John Doe probe.

At one time, more than a half dozen authors had books in the works on the Bembenek case. Only two, however, were published, and both maintained Bembenek's innocence.

After more than a decade behind bars, Bembenek finally won her freedom in 1992 when she agreed to plead no contest to a reduced charged of second-degree murder.

Three TV movies later, some cracks began to appear in the Bembenek fable. Nick Gugliatto complained that he was abandoned by his lover immediately after their arrest. Ira Robins also had become disenchanted with his heroine. He had hoped some of the big movie money might help defray some of his expenses over the years. Like Gugliatto, she apparently dropped Robins when he wasn't useful to her anymore.

After her release, Bembenek went on a speaking tour, proclaiming her innocence and calling for more educational opportunities for inmates. But she had difficulty finding a job, working for an accounting firm until it closed and then for temporary employment agencies.

In February 1996, Bembenek was back in jail, arrested in a drug investigation. She was held on a parole violation, and a drug test showed she had used marijuana. After two weeks in jail, she was released but required to wear an electronic monitoring bracelet. She was diagnosed with hepatitis C, a liver ailment, and underwent treatment for depression.

By July 1996, Bembenek had tired of her notoriety. She moved to Washington state, where her parents lived, and looked forward to living "someplace where nobody knows who I am." Her mother, Virginia, said the move was a matter of life and death due to her daughter's depression and suicidal thoughts.

The most telling evidence against Bembenek came from

her own attorney. During a television interview, Eisenberg said, "Everything I know about points to the fact she did do it." The comment provided part of the basis for Bembenek's appeal, and led to the revocation of Eisenberg's law license in Wisconsin.

Did Lawrencia Bembenek put on her green jogging suit and kill Christine Schultz that night? Or was she an innocent woman framed for a brutal crime? It's a mystery that may never be resolved.

72.
What's killing the bald eagles?
Wisconsin, 1995

After years of pesticide use drove them away, bald eagles returned to the Wisconsin River during the winter in the late 1970s and early 1980s after DDT was banned.

Eagles ingested DDT when they ate fish contaminated when the pesticide washed into the water. DDT caused eagle egg shells to become so thin that the birds could not hatch.

By 1995, a new threat was killing the eagles. A mystery illness afflicted sixteen eagles during the winter of 1994-95, killing fourteen of them. The eagles had convulsions, seizures and vomited before they died.

Scientists believed the killer was some kind of toxin ingested by the eagles. But research ruled out the cause as heavy metals, polychlorinated biphenyls (PCBs), phosphates, bacteria, fungus, parasites and viruses.

Some scientists attributed the disease to a mild Wisconsin winter that year.

But by 2000, the mysterious toxin, which caused lesions

in the brain, apparently was killing eagles in four southern states. The malady, named avian brain lesion syndrome, killed 30 eagles over a five-year period.

The actual number of deaths are relatively small compared to the nearly 600 pairs of nesting bald eagles in Wisconsin. The toxin-related illness appeared as eagles were about to be removed from the endangered species list.

What is the mysterious toxin that's presenting a new threat to the American symbol?

73.
Who killed
Officer Finlay Beaton?
Superior, 1919

Superior Police Officer Finlay Beaton was killed over a ham and two chickens. That was the loot collected by the robbers who shot him to death on July 27, 1919.

Beaton was patrolling a commercial area along Tower Avenue when he apparently heard the sound of a blast coming from a supermarket. Four officers were within a block of the market when the safe door was blown, but Beaton was the only one to hear the blast. He was about to walk into an alley at the rear of the market when he was shot to death.

Patrolman Martin Widness was the first officer on the scene.

"I heard several shots fired," he told the *Superior Telegram*. "I knew there were at least four."

Widness found Beaton lying in a pool of blood, but the robbers had disappeared. Beaton had suffered a fatal wound in the head and also was struck in the left leg by

.45-caliber bullets.

Hillary St. John, who lived nearby, told police he saw several men with flashlights in the alley behind the market and assumed they were plainclothes police officers. Later, St. John said he heard gunshots, then a car roared away. The robbers were seen leaving in a seven-passenger Mitchell auto with Wisconsin plates.

A ham and two chickens were found at the rear of the market, but the burglars left in a hurry without their loot.

With the number of suspects, and the fact that all appeared in their early twenties, it's incredible that none ever came forward to confess or implicate one of their accomplices in the murder.

74.
Why did a Harmony Grove family die?
Lodi, 1998

Harmony Grove is a rural community near Lodi and Lake Wisconsin, in southern Columbia County. In August 1998, three family members died of carbon monoxide poisoning in a case that authorities found difficult to determine whether it was accidental, suicide or murder.

No suicide note was found and there was no sign of a struggle. But Cheryl Cady, 45, was found dead along with her son, Cory Cole, 20, and daughter, Bria Meitner, 11.

The Cady car was left running in the basement garage, and the poisonous fumes drifted to the bedrooms upstairs, killing the family.

Detectives interviewed many people who knew the Cady family and conducted tests, running the Cady car again in the basement garage in similar hot summer weather to determine how long it would take for the poisonous fumes to overcome the victims.

Were the Cady deaths the result of a clever plot to murder the family? Was a family member distraught enough to kill everyone in a suicide? Or did someone simply neglect to shut off the car?

75.
Who killed Dorothy Raczkowski?

Friendship, 1989

Dorothy Raczkowski, 60, lived alone in a white wood-frame house near the intersection of two country roads near the western edge of Adams County. On her 240-acre farm, she raised black Angus cattle and chickens and grew hay. She also worked the evening shift sorting potatoes at Ore-Ida Foods in Plover.

Adams County, one of the state's poorest areas, is not far from the popular recreation area of Wisconsin Dells. During the mid-1970's, eight people were murdered during a two-year period.

Raczkowski was found dead about 8:15 a.m. Nov. 17, 1989 on her garage floor in a pool of blood, apparently the victim of blows to the head.

Stanley Buchanan, who found the body, said he believed she was hit on the head by an intruder when she stepped inside the garage's side door to open the larger door for her car. She probably was attacked when she returned home from her 3-to-11 p.m. shift.

Buchanan said the garage lights, car's engine and car lights were off when he arrived.

Robbery didn't appear to be the motive because a purse containing money was left behind in the car and nothing was missing from the house.

76.

Who killed Patrolman Grant Dosch

Madison, 1918

Grant Dosch was a young police officer who had served about two years on the force. He worked the graveyard shift, patrolling the Schenk's Corners area on Madison's East Side, and was on his way home on February 4, 1918, when he noticed something suspicious going on at a store along West Washington Avenue.

Thieves had entered the rear door of the store, using carpenter chisels to force the door open. The general merchandise store was owned by Louis Cohen.

Dosch apparently pulled his revolver from his pocket and tried to arrest one of the burglars. Before he could take the man into custody, Dosch was shot by an accomplice across the street.

Two shots were fired. One hit Dosch above his right eye, the other shattered his jawbone. A shotgun with both barrels loaded was found across the street. Police believed the gun was fired and reloaded before the thieves fled. A wagon loaded with stolen merchandise was found in a vacant barn in the same block.

It wasn't the shots that awakened Elmer Currie of 756 W. Washington Avenue. He heard Dosch groaning and found the young officer on the sidewalk. His unfired and loaded revolver was found at his side. His gloves and cap were a few feet away in the snow. Currie said he found no one else around when he discovered the officer.

Dosch died seven hours later at St. Mary's Hospital, where he was treated by Dr. Joseph P. Dean. He left behind a wife and two children.

Eight police officers were assigned to the case, but the cold-blooded killer of young Patrolman Dosch never was found.

77.
Who killed Dorothy Laws?
Milwaukee, 1989

Dorothy Laws, 24, was found dead Nov. 18, 1989, in the basement of an unoccupied house in the 2800 block of North 18th Street. She died of blunt force trauma and head injuries.

Laws was the third of a dozen black women murdered on Milwaukee's North Side over a decade from the mid-1980s to the mid-1990s. Many of the women were involved in prostitution and crack cocaine.

George L. "Mule" Jones was linked to several of the murders and pleaded guilty to one of them. He was not charged in the other cases, but admitted "dope dating" some of the women and trading drugs for sex.

A city worker with expertise in knot-tying was questioned in some of the other murders in which the victims were tied up with rope or clothesline. He was never charged.

78.
Did UFOs visit Belleville?
Belleville, 1987

Police officer Glen Kazmar couldn't believe what he was seeing — flashing red, blue and white lights in the sky that looked like they were from out of this world.

About 3 a.m. on Jan. 15, 1987, Kazmer and his ride-along passenger, Jeff Furseth, drove to a hill along Quarry Road outside the Belleville village limits to get a better look. They called O'Hare International Airport in Chicago, which confirmed there was an object on their radar screen that they couldn't identify.

Kazmer and Furseth were joined by other deputies from Dane and Green counties. They watched the lights for nearly an hour before whatever it was sped away.

Three months later, on March 6, Harvey Funseth, a surveyor for the state transportation department, was driving south on Highway 69 with Fred Gochenauer when they saw strange box-shaped objects in the sky near Paoli, a small community not far from Belleville. Funseth later said he saw a large rectangle hovering over three smaller similar-shaped objects.

He watched as the largest object turned and headed toward him. When the object got closer, he saw that it was shaped like a torpedo or airplane fuselage without wings. The object, which had a pair of blinking lights in the rear, stopped above their heads. Funseth took ten pictures of it with his 35-millimeter camera. But the pictures of the object didn't turn out, even though other shots on the same roll turned out fine.

A few minutes later, Lavonne Freidig, who knew Funseth, saw the same shapes as she looked out her back door on Belleville's north side.

Funseth said two men in dark suits visited his home about a month after the sightings. They claimed to be investigating the sightings, but refused to reveal their identities. He said they asked him for details, then tried to persuade him that he never saw anything.

The Belleville sightings were among an estimated two hundred similar incidents that have occurred in Wisconsin. But they were enough to earn a monicker for the village: "UFO Capital of the World." The village holds a UFO Day every year where participants often come dressed as aliens. So far, the celebration hasn't lured back any other-world visitors.

Were the strange objects seen in Belleville from another world? Were they part of some covert military exercise? Who were the men in black who visited Funseth? Those mysteries remain.

79.
Who killed Susan LeMahieu?

Madison, 1979

Susan LeMahieu disappeared ten days before Christmas 1979 from her room at Allen Hall on Madison's State Street, then a residential center for the developmentally disabled.

A 1974 graduate of Madison East High School, LeMahieu, 24, was mildly retarded and physically handicapped. In 1966, when she was age ten, two of her brothers died acci-

dentally when they suffocated in an abandoned refrigerator in the basement of the family's home.

Her body was found in the dense brush of a marsh about 150 feet from a parking lot in the University of Wisconsin Arboretum.

Susan LeMahieu

80.

Who killed Terryl Stanford?

Beloit, 1994

A worker was cleaning the parking lot behind the Naughty But Nice Adult Bookstore on Aug. 24, 1994, when he discovered a woman's body in some overgrown brush.

Toxicology tests determined the barefoot woman had died 12 to 24 hours earlier. No gunshot wounds or stab wounds were found on the body. Investigators couldn't determine the cause of death, and failed to come up with any suspects.

Through a tattoo, investigators identified the dead woman as Terryl J. Stanford, 29, of Chicago. She had numerous prostitution arrests and was known to frequent Chicago area truck stops.

Rock County Sheriff Joe Black said he wasn't sure whether Stanford was killed at the scene or whether her body was dumped under the adult bookstore's sign by someone traveling along the interstate.

Detectives thought they had a break in the case in 1996 when an East Coast man confessed to slayings of prostitutes around the country. But the man had an alibi for the time that Stanford was killed.

Stanford wouldn't be the only woman whose body was found near the adult bookstore. Three years later, decayed remains of another woman, still unidentified, were discovered in the same location.

81.

Who killed Berit Beck?

Waupun, 1990

Berit Beck, 18, vanished while driving to a computer training seminar in Appleton on July 17, 1990. Her van was found in a Fond du Lac parking lot, but it would be more than a month before her body was found in a ditch near Waupun.

An autopsy confirmed that the young woman died of asphyxiation, but provided few clues about why she was killed or who the killer was. Lt. Ed Sheppard of the Fond du Lac County sheriff's department said the decomposition of the body destroyed valuable evidence.

Five thousand people attended Berit Beck's funeral in Racine. Cars were decorated with pink ribbons, symbolizing the hope her friends and relatives once had that she would be found alive.

She had written down the mileage on her van before leaving Sturtevant for the trip to Appleton because she expected to be reimbursed for the mileage. When her van was found, the odometer showed 462 miles more than would be involved in a direct trip from Sturtevant to Fond du Lac.

Detectives soon focused on a 30-year-old convicted bank robber who was seen near a shopping center when Beck's van was recovered. The suspect later served time in federal prison.

In 1994, Berit's mother, Diane, held a memorial service for her daughter at Racine Bible Church. She said she hoped to bring public attention to the case.

"Someone needs to be punished for this," Diane Beck said. "I can't understand why someone would want to hurt such a beautiful girl."

A year later, an Illinois man was questioned in the murder of Berit Beck and the disappearance of Laurie Depies. Larry D. Hall of Wabash, Indiana, was accused of kidnapping a fifteen-year-old girl and killing her. Investigators said Hall had come to Wisconsin during the time period when the two cases occurred.

82.

How big is Richardson's cave?

Middleton, 1845

John McDonald Jr. was the first man to enter a mysterious cave west of Madison in 1845. According to a 1947 account in the Verona Centennial Souvenir, McDonald, who entered the cave about 8 a.m., was lost for hours and didn't emerge until late afternoon.

The complex cave, believed to be at least several stories deep, on the David Richardson farm has many levels that still remain unexplored. Geologists have mapped about a thousand feet of the cave descending forty feet underground, but say the mapped portion isn't large enough to hold the thousands of gallons of runoff water that pour into the cave each spring.

Richardson was the first farmer who settled the area in 1851. For decades, the cave was known as the Great Cave of Dane County.

The largest natural cave in Wisconsin is about two thousand feet long on Horseshoe Bay in Door County. But Richardson's cave, part of which has filled with mud, could be even bigger if all of it could be explored.

Although their parents likely discouraged it, youngsters often played in the cave's opening, building bonfires and telling ghost stories. They'd sometimes watch pigs get stuck in sink holes when underground caverns would collapse.

Several years ago, explorers discovered a "bone room," where small animals apparently went to hibernate in the fall, then were trapped by water in the spring.

The cave is difficult to explore because of a bottleneck usually filled with water, about three feet inside. The only way to get beyond it is to swim under water.

In 1969, some people wanted to dam up the water flow so Richardson's cave could be explored completely before it disappeared. But the damming never took place.

83.
Who killed Debra Ann Maniece?
Milwaukee, 1994

Debra Ann Maniece, 31, was found dead Nov. 20, 1994, in an abandoned building in the 1900 block of North 12th Street on Milwaukee's North Side.

In one of the most vicious of a series of a dozen murders of black women on the city's North Side, Maniece had been strangled and beaten with a brick. Many of the dozen victims were prostitutes who used crack cocaine.

George L. "Mule" Jones pleaded guilty to murdering one of the women and was sentenced to life in prison. He also admitted that he knew some of the other victims and had "dope dated" them in which he gave them drugs for sex.

A man who worked for the city of Milwaukee, who was an expert in knots, was questioned but never charged in other cases where the victims had been tied up.

84.

Was the Tallman house haunted?

Horicon, 1988

By late January 1988, Debi and Allen Tallman had enough. They packed up their possessions and moved with their two children out of their three-year-old house at 415 Larabee in Horicon. They lost three thousand dollars by letting their house revert to the mortgage company.

The Tallmans claimed their home was haunted. They had heard voices and seen balls of fire glowing in their garage. Their children, ages two and three, saw the ghost of a woman surrounded by flames in a doorway of the home.

When the story of Horicon's haunted house was publicized, thousands of visitors descended on the quiet small-town street to see if they could spot a ghost. Local businesses took advantage of the sudden influx of tourism. A local bakery began peddling ghost cupcakes and a "Poltergeese" T-shirt was produced, playing upon Horicon's reputation as the gateway to Horicon marsh, where thousands of Canada geese assemble each fall for their trip south.

Police officers were more concerned that someone was trying to play a hoax on the Tallmans. They barricaded the street and checked the house for hidden microphones or movie projectors. The police hired an electrical engineer to go through the home.

Parapsychologists also visited the home and concluded the house likely was haunted by spirits. Others, however, speculated that perhaps a gas leak might have fired the family's imaginations. The Tallmans rejected a lucrative offer by the *National Enquirer* newspaper to publicize their story.

The Tallmans decided the source of their ghost problems was a set of secondhand bunk beds they had bought a few months before. They buried the bunk beds in a landfill, where they could be sure no one would ever build a home. They had no further problems with spirits haunting their new home in Beaver Dam.

Another family moved into the Horicon house and also had no problems with ghosts or unexplained occurrences. The public fervor over the haunted house dissipated. The Tallmans sold their story to Michael Norman of River Falls, author of *Haunted America* and other ghost-related books, and to the television show "Unsolved Mysteries."

A year after the Tallmans moved out, Wisconsin Power & Light Co., now Alliant Energy, replaced faulty gas fittings at some homes in Horicon. But a company spokesman said no faulty fittings were found at the Larabee house.

Paul Kurtz, of the Committee for the Scientific Investigation of the Paranormal, based in Buffalo, New York, said the haunting claims by the Tallmans were similar to many cases in which people misinterpret normal events, then are hunted down and offered money by book publishers and television producers.

Was the Tallman house haunted? Were the bunk beds linked somehow to the ghost? Or were the strange occurrences simply the result of leaking natural gas?

85.
Who killed Erik Kraemer?
Comstock, 1999

Erik Kraemer was an honor student and a popular athlete at Turtle Lake High School. In the spring of 1999, he set a record for running 400 meters.

A few months later, on the evening of Aug. 7, 1999, Kraemer, 17, was nearing the end of a five-mile run around Pipe Lake, where his family lived, when he was shot to death. The young man's body was found by a passing motorist.

A $10,000 reward was established for information leading to the arrest and conviction of the killer. But the case puzzled police investigators, who were unable to find a motive for the killing and could not identify a suspect.

The case terrified Kraemer's classmates in the peaceful communities of northern Wisconsin. Was a killer stalking high school students? Would he strike again? John McGrath said his daughter, Amanda, a classmate of Kraemer's, refused to sleep in her downstairs bedroom.

"It's scared the hell out of my kids that this guy is still running around," McGrath said. "This hasn't been forgotten. This has to be resolved."

By January 2000, police got a tip that a 19-year-old acquaintance of Kraemer's from New Richmond might be involved in the shooting. Investigators planned to search his home and interview him about the murder.

Before he could be questioned, the man shot himself to death at his family's home, leaving the case unresolved.

"From the information we have, he was aware we were

investigating him," said Lt. Dave Lindholm of the Polk County Sheriff's Department.

Did the man shoot Erik Kraemer that summer evening? Or was it someone else?

86.
Who killed Sheila Farrior?
Milwaukee, 1995

Shelia Farrior, 36, was found strangled June 27, 1995, in the bedroom of a vacant house in the 1400 block of West Chambers Street on Milwaukee's North Side.

Farrior, who left five children without a mother, was among a dozen black Milwaukee women murdered on the city's North Side over a decade. She also was a member of the Friendship Club, a center that offered counseling to drug addicts.

Sandy Farrior, her father, was among relatives of the victims who criticized the police for their failure to solve the murders.

"Obviously, I can't say it was given a high priority," Farrior told the *Milwaukee Journal-Sentinel* in 1997. "They can't do anything for my daughter, but maybe they can prevent the deaths of others."

87.

Did the Mexican Mafia kill C.D. Jackson?

Beloit, 1994

When C.D. Jackson of Beloit failed to show up for his trial on domestic abuse charges, no one imagined he had been murdered and his body dumped along a rural Rock County road.

A county highway worker found Jackson's body about 2:30 p.m. Dec. 5, 1994.

Jackson, 42, had been arrested three months earlier after a fight with his girlfriend, and he was charged with battery, criminal damage to property and criminal trespass. A jury trial was scheduled to begin the day his body was found. When he didn't show up, a judge issued a warrant for Jackson's arrest.

After an investigation, police decided Jackson was murdered over a drug deal gone bad by three men who described themselves as the Mexican Mafia. They were Jose Marquez, 33, of Rockford, Illinois, Ruperto Luna, 38, of Beloit; and Walter Sago, 40, of Beloit.

Marquez and Luna were charged with kidnapping, false imprisonment and conspiracy to deliver cocaine. Sago was charged with conspiracy to deliver cocaine.

But as a trial for Marquez was about to begin, charges were dropped against all three suspects. Rock County District Attorney Scott McCarthy said his key witness, Miguel Valdez Rivera, was a "brazen liar" and McCarthy said he couldn't put Rivera on the stand.

Was C.D. Jackson murdered over a drug deal by the Mexican Mafia? The case remains unsolved.

88.
How many people did Ed Gein kill?
Plainfield, 1957

Ed Gein, who lived on a farm near Plainfield, Wisconsin, is one of the world's most notorious murderers, and the inspiration for several movies, including "Psycho" and "The Texas Chainsaw Massacre."

But only two murders actually were credited to Gein. On Nov. 16, 1957, Gein went to buy a gallon of anti-freeze at a Plainfield hardware store operated by Bernice Worden. While waiting for her to pump out the liquid, he inspected a gun for sale and shot her in the back of the head.

Police found Worden's disemboweled, headless body hanging like a deer in Gein's woodshed. They also found the face and head of Mary Hogan, who had disappeared three years earlier from the Pine Grove tavern, which she operated about six miles from Gein's farm.

Gein's farmhouse had no electricity, no gas and no telephone. He read girlie magazines by the light of a kerosene lamp. The nine-room farmhouse was strewn with body parts and had the stench of embalming fluid except the bedroom of Gein's mother, which he kept neat as a shrine to the woman who had died twelve years earlier.

Gein robbed at least ten graves, taking the body parts back home where he made masks, costumes, lamp shades and chair seats from human skin. He would dance under the moonlight wearing female masks and other body parts.

He said that after his mother died, "I wanted to become a woman."

Gein told investigators his unnatural attachment to his mother grew into obsessions with sex that led to grave-robbing and the two grisly murders.

Authorities were reluctant to dig up the graves where Gein said he had gotten his body parts. Finally, under public pressure, they dug up four of them and found that the bodies had been removed.

When detectives questioned Gein, they found him agreeable and willing to admit to nearly any murder they suggested. He became a suspect in the disappearances of eight-year-old Georgia Jean Weckler in 1947, teenage babysitter Evelyn Hartley from La Crosse in 1953, and in the butcher slaying of sixteen-year-old Judith Anderson of Chicago.

But these murders all involved girls and the victims of Gein's two proven murders and grave-robbing were middle-aged. Some people also suspected he killed tavern operator Cad Bates near Wisconsin Rapids in 1952.

Gein was judged insane and never went to trial. He died of natural causes in 1984, while still a patient at Mendota Mental Health Institute in Madison. He was buried in Spiritland Cemetery in Plainfield, where he had robbed graves three decades earlier. Judge Robert Gollmar, who had ruled on Gein's sanity, described him as the most unique criminal ever with the largest collection of women's body parts in the world.

The fascination with Gein's grisly crimes and lifestyle continues today and in 2000 his tombstone was stolen, possibly by a Gein memorabilia collector.

Did some of Gein's body parts come from living victims other than Mary Hogan and Bernice Worden? Because

Gein could not be questioned easily by authorities, and because his case never went to trial, no one will ever know for sure.

89.
Who killed Lorrie L. Huebner?
Janesville, 1990

Rock County Coroner Richard McCaul first determined that Lorrie Huebner, 27, of Janesville, died of natural causes when she was found dead. Later, a state pathologist found she had been suffocated or strangled.

Huebner's husband, Dale, said he noticed blood on her face the morning of Jan. 8, 1990, when he tried to wake her up. But he figured it was caused by problems with her hearing aid. He decided to let her sleep, and finally called the police when he couldn't rouse her about noon.

A grand jury hearing failed to bring charges even after one of two suspects bragged that he had put Huebner "six feet under."

No wounds were found on the woman's body, although she had a rash that she frequently experienced because she was allergic to cats and some of the jewelry she wore.

District Attorney Perry Folts closed the case after detectives were unable to conduct extensive interviews with the two suspects.

90.

What happened to Gregg Kammer?

Milwaukee, 1985

As a young man, Gregg Kammer was an entrepreneur. He sold hot dogs at Madison sporting events and sold falafel from a pushcart on the University of Wisconsin's Library Mall.

He became the youngest board member ever of Madison's Beth Israel Center, and spent summers as a counselor at the Jewish-sponsored Ramah youth camp  near Eagle River. Among his hobbies were coin collecting and sculpting. In 1976, the Madison Memorial High School student was awarded a $1,000 scholarship and named a Bicentennial Senior in a national competition.

Until June 21, 1985, Gregg Kammer seemed to have a great life ahead of him. That was the day he disappeared.

Greg Kammer

By that time, Kammer had married and moved to Milwaukee, where he started a business called Honor Snacks, which sold candy bars, potato chips, juices and health food on the honor system at Milwaukee businesses.

On that first day of summer, Kammer left his Milwaukee office and planned to return an hour later. The car he was driving was found three days later at O'Hare Airport in Chicago, but Kammer had vanished.

"It's not like a kid who was freaked out on drugs or flaked out got lost,' his mother, Bonnie, told a *Wisconsin State Journal* reporter in 1986. "It's more like a Boy Scout disappeared."

Kammer's wife, Phyllis Post-Kammer, visited Israel in 1987, hoping to find a clue to her missing husband's whereabouts. She came back disappointed.

Did Gregg Kammer have secrets that his mother didn't know about? Did he vanish to start a new life somewhere else? Or was he murdered?

91.
Who killed Yvonne Reynolds?
Milwaukee, 1995

Yvonne Reynolds, 40, was found dead Sept. 1, 1995, in a pile of clothes in a bedroom of an apartment in the 2600 block of North Richards Street on Milwaukee's North Side. She died of manual strangulation.

Reynolds was missing for three weeks before her body was discovered.

When Reynolds was murdered, then-Milwaukee Police Chief Philip Arreola said there was no evidence to link seven slayings of black women on the North Side.

"We are reviewing each and every one of these cases individually and collectively," he said. "I cannot quickly jump to a conclusion based on impulse or hysteria."

Arreola's defense of the department's handling of the cases came after two aldermen blasted the police and said the cases hadn't been given high priority because the slain women were black.

Later, as the number of victims mounted to a dozen, the FBI would be called in to assist. George L. "Mule" Jones was linked to some of the cases, especially those like Reynolds where the victim was strangled with the killer's bare hands.

Jones pleaded guilty to killing one of the women and received a life sentence. Many of the women were involved in prostitution, and Jones admitted "dope dating" some of them in which he gave them drugs for sex.

A city worker familiar with knots was questioned in some of the other murders, but never charged.

92.
What happened to Jeanette Zapata?
Madison, 1976

Jeanette Zapata loved to fly. She first got interested in flying when her father took her for an airplane ride in October 1955.

She got her pilot's license at age 16 and later, after marrying Eugene Zapata, she taught him to fly.

In October 1976, Jeanette Zapata sent her three children off to school. It was the last anyone saw of her.

The Zapatas were in the throes of a divorce at the time, but police found no evidence of foul play.

Eugene Zapata told a *Wisconsin State Journal* reporter that his wife was spotted by airline employees in Madison and St. Louis. He believed she decided to vanish and create a new identity, using the services of a Champaign, Illinois company that specialized in creating new identities for people.

"It may have been just the pressure of it because I filed

for custody of the kids," said Eugene Zapata, who remarried after his wife's disappearance. "She was a very strong-willed person. If she made up her mind that she wanted to disappear, she could do it."

Did Jeanette Zapata fly away to a new life somewhere under a new identity? Or did someone get away with murder?

93.
Who killed Mark Genna?

Madison, 1992

Mark Genna was a disabled man and that made his brutal murder in February 1992 even more difficult to fathom.

Genna died in his apartment on Madison's South Side after suffering several blows to the head with some kind of blunt instrument like a baseball bat or club. Police said the weapon, which wasn't recovered, probably was heavier than a bat because of the damage it did.

Police were left with few clues. They believed that burglary or robbery was the motive, but the thieves showed uncharacteristic viciousness especially to a man who couldn't adequately defend himself.

Missing from Genna's apartment was cash left from a Social Security check he had received the same day he was murdered. Genna's father, Anthony, estimated his son probably had a couple hundred dollars.

Genna had a roommate, but police ruled him out as a suspect. A year after the murder, detectives identified a suspect in police reports submitted to the district attorney. But District Attorney William Foust said there wasn't enough evidence to prosecute.

If the killer ever is found, Anthony Genna said he could

think of a better form of justice than bringing him to trial.

"If they ever catch that son of a bitch, I hope they let me in the room with him for a few minutes with a baseball bat," the angry father told a *Wisconsin State Journal* reporter in 1992.

94.

Who was the woman found behind the bookstore?

Beloit, 1997

When the woman's body was found in March 1997 near the Naughty But Nice Adult Bookstore near Interstate 90 in Rock County, the body was so badly decomposed that authorities still haven't been able to identify her.

But the body was found at the same spot where the body of a Chicago woman was found three years earlier.

Someone picking up debris at a nearby campground spotted the decomposed remains about 1 p.m. in a wooded area that separates the back lot of the bookstore from Turtle Creek Campground. At the time, investigators predicted that identification of the second body would take several weeks. But even that proved optimistic.

Rock County investigators commissioned a forensic sculptor to do a rendering of how the woman may have looked. Photos of the rendering were distributed to law enforcement agencies.

The dead woman was described as white, between 19 and 30 years old, between 5 feet 4 inches and 5 feet 7 inches tall with light to medium-brown shoulder-length hair.

Are the two deaths related? Is a serial killer on the loose

with perverted sexual fantasies that lead him to kill women and dump their bodies behind the adult bookstore? The truth may never be known.

95.
Who killed Wanda Harris?
Milwaukee, 1997

Wanda Harris, 38, was found beaten and strangled Nov. 9, 1997, under several old tires in the 2000 block of West Fond du Lac Avenue on Milwaukee's North Side.

She was one of a dozen Milwaukee black women killed over a decade, most of whom were involved in prostitution. Although George L. "Mule" Jones was linked to some of the killings and convicted of one of them, he was in the Milwaukee County Jail when Harris was killed.

Harris had arrests dating back two decades. Her most recent had been for possession of a tube used for smoking crack cocaine. She also was convicted of offering a sex act to an undercover officer for $20.

96.
Why did Vickie Omernick die?
Merrill, 1994

Vickie Omernick planned to celebrate her 28th birthday on June 4, 1994, on a weekend camping and fishing trip with her husband. Instead, she died in a bizarre explosion inside a camper mounted on the back of a pickup truck.

Ronald Omernick, a Wausau firefighter, told investigators he was about to park the truck at a fishing spot at

Prairie Dells Park, about nine miles north of Merrill, when Vickie called through the connecting window that she was going to light the kerosene lantern.

The last thing Omernick recalled seeing was a bright flash from the camper before he was knocked unconscious by an explosion. When he awoke, Omernick said he was on the ground and the truck was engulfed in flames. The fire was so intense that only the shell of the pickup truck was left.

Omernick said he lost consciousness again, then awoke about 5 a.m. He wandered to a nearby home and reported the incident to police.

The truck had rolled about forty feet down a rocky embankment into a deep ravine. Police said Omernick may have been thrown from the truck as it rolled.

The couple's two children, ages four and six, had been left with relatives.

Propane used for a stove in the camper probably ignited during the explosion. But why hadn't Vickie, who rode in the camper to the fishing spot, smelled a leak?

When coroner David Haskins filled out the death certificate for Vickie Omernick, he didn't answer questions about the date, location and time of her death, leaving those questions blank.

97.

Who killed Virginia Hendrickson?

Janesville, 1988

Virginia Bothum Hendrickson liked to party with a lot of different men. She lived with a few of them, and met others at The Zoo, a Janesville tavern.

When she was found dead on June 5, 1988, it was difficult to pinpoint a single suspect. In the brutal slaying, her head was nearly severed from her body. Blood was splattered through the house and Amanda, her 1-year-old daughter, was found crying in a crib upstairs.

She had been stabbed more than 40 times in the back, neck and head. A trail of blood was found on the sidewalk leading to a neighbor's house.

Virginia grew up near Cambridge, the youngest of six children. Her first child, Travis, was born premature in 1985 and died at the age of five months. She was married for less than two months to Phillip Hendrickson, Amanda's father.

Police believe Virginia may have confronted someone outside the house, then went inside.

David LaFleur Jr., one of her former roommates, said Virginia was drunk every day. She had no job and collected welfare. She would meet men at The Zoo and disappear with them for a while, leaving her daughter in the care of anyone in the bar. A bar manager said she believed Virginia was working as a prostitute.

LaFleur was questioned about the murder, and others told police he had called them to try to set up an alibi. LaFleur told detectives he might have been involved in the murder, but couldn't remember because he had been taking pain medication.

Another former roommate, Dean Paulson, said he and Wanda Finch stopped at Virginia's house to check on some of his property in her garage on the night before her body was found.

Paulson said he saw an orange or red Pontiac Firebird pull out of Virginia's garage. He saw Virginia's car, a Chrysler Cordoba, parked in her driveway, parallel to the house.

When police arrived six hours later, the Cordoba was parked in a different place.

Paulson and Finch were two of many people questioned about the murder. Finch had a fight with Virginia a few days before the murder.

Paulson said Stephen Maas, another former roommate, threatened Virginia a few weeks before her death. Maas threatened to kill her after she kicked over his motorcycle, according to Paulson.

Detectives tried to unravel Virginia's tangled web of relationships but were unable to find out who was responsible for her savage murder.

98.
Who killed Rasheda Dickerson?
Milwaukee, 1996

Rasheda Dickerson, 17, was found strangled and wrapped in a quilt near the North Avenue dam on March 11, 1996, on Milwaukee's North Side. A "clove hitch" was used to tie her up.

She was one of a dozen black Milwaukee women killed between the mid-1980s and mid-1990s.

A Milwaukee man familiar with knot-tying was questioned in the deaths of some of the other women but police didn't have enough evidence to charge him with murder.

Another man, George L. "Mule" Jones, confessed to one of the murders and was implicated in several others in which the women had been strangled with the killer's bare hands instead of rope or clothesline.

99.
Who killed Shirley Stewart?
Madison, 1980

Shirley Stewart, 17, disappeared January 2, 1980, after finishing her shift at the Dean Clinic, where she worked as a maid. Her body was found by four archaeology students mapping a state park in July 1981 in a densely wooded area of the town of Westport, north of Madison. Brush was piled over the body in an apparent effort to conceal it.

An autopsy was unable to determine the cause of death. Coroner Clyde Chamberlain said evidence couldn't be found of a bullet or knife wound, and she possibly could have been strangled.

Stewart was among seven women abducted and murdered in the Madison area over a dozen years. All of the killings probably weren't committed by the same suspect, but Stewart's murder is similar to several other cases in which women disappeared and later their bodies were found in secluded rural areas.

Serial killer Henry Lee Lucas confessed to two of the murders, but later recanted his confession. Detectives found evidence that Lucas and his sidekick Ottis Toole may have come through the Madison area to visit relatives.

100.
Who killed the Balzer family?
Sauk City, 1922

Mary Balzer and her two brothers, Julius and William, were deeply religious. They also had investment in the stock and bond markets, and didn't seem to have any enemies.

In 1922, the three family members were clubbed to death in a brutal murder that shocked the community. Their house was ransacked and police were unable to identify a suspect.

Five years later, William Coffey was arrested for clubbing his wife, Hattie Sherman Hales, to death near Platteville. He killed her not only for her money, but also to cover up the fact that he already was married to another woman.

William Coffey

Coffey had served time in prison for stealing money from another woman whom he claimed falsely accused him after he refused to marry her. He also was a bond salesman who preyed upon religious people like the Balzers.

Due to the brutality of the murder of Coffey's bigamous wife, detectives theorized that Coffey probably had killed before.

They determined that Coffey had been in the Sauk City area at the time of the Balzer murders, and he admitted he'd read about the case in the newspaper.

Coffey admitted killing his bigamous wife and confessed he toyed with women's affections to take advantage of them. But he denied killing the Balzer family.

He was sentenced to life in prison for killing his wife and died at Waupun State Prison in 1962. The hope for solving the Balzer murders may have died with him.

Did William Coffey savagely murder the Balzer family? Or was it someone else?

101.

Was Jeffrey Dahmer crazy?

Milwaukee, 1991

After his gruesome crimes were discovered in July 1991, Jeffrey Dahmer calmly offered details about his killing spree to detectives in exchange for cigarettes.

Dahmer was the worst serial killer in Wisconsin history. He admitted killing seventeen men and boys. He had sex with some of the victims after death, ate some of the body parts and, in the worst living nightmare out of a horror movie, tried to lobotomize some of his victims by drilling holes in their heads and freezing parts of the brains so he could keep them alive for his own sexual pleasure. Five skulls and other body parts were found in Dahmer's Milwaukee apartment, along with a cooler

An unsettling aspect to the Dahmer case, however, was that he saw no weird visions, didn't receive commands from voices in his head, and showed no signs of schizophrenia.

Through it all, Dahmer's appearance and composure belied the savagery of his acts. Far from a raging madman, he appeared to comprehend his situation. He made no claim of mind control by aliens or the devil. During hours of interrogation by police, he was calm, polite and generally cooperative. Most of the details about his crimes came from his own recollections and admissions.

Dahmer's dissection, cannibalism and necrophilia rivaled the murder and grave robbing of Ed Gein more than three decades earlier. Unlike Gein, however, Dahmer had no readily apparent mental illness. But how could a man commit such atrocities if he were sane? The answer didn't come easily.

At Dahmer's trial in February 1992, expert testimony centered on whether the serial killer met the requirements of Wisconsin's insanity law. In order to be judged insane, it had to be proven that he wasn't aware of the wrongfulness of his acts.

Forensic psychiatrists testifying for the prosecution and defense gave their views about whether Dahmer was insane. Focusing on the narrow standards of the law, however, the psychiatrists at the trial failed to deal with the larger questions of how a man could commit such inhuman acts and lead a normal appearing life at the same time.

One answer was provided by Dr. Gary Maier, a Madison forensic psychiatrist who provided consultation for *Massacre in Milwaukee,* one of the books about the Dahmer case. Maier compared Dahmer to doctors in Nazi Germany who were able to kill in the name of healing. Both suffered from what Maier called a doubling of personalities, allowing two conflicting sets of ethics to operate simultaneously.

Dahmer was found sane and convicted of fifteen of the

murders. He also was convicted of an earlier murder in Ohio and began serving fifteen consecutive life terms at Columbia Correctional Institution in Portage.

On November 28, 1994, Dahmer and another inmate were in the prison gymnasium working on a cleaning detail when they were brutally attacked by inmate Christopher J. Scarver, who had been working with them. Dahmer and the other inmate, Jesse Anderson, were bludgeoned to death.

The question of Dahmer's sanity, however, lingered after his death. His mother, Joyce Flint, of Fresno, California, wanted his brain preserved so it could be studied to determine whether biological factors caused his criminal behavior. But his father, Lionel Dahmer, of Akron, Ohio, wanted the brain cremated. His father won in court and the brain was destroyed.

Was the calm and polite serial killer crazy? The question may never be answered with certainty.

Index

Symbols

602 Club 86, 124

A

Adams County 65, 73, 75, 135
Adams County Memorial Hospital
    75
Allen Hall 139
American Brass Company 66
"America's Most Wanted" 130
Amherst, Wisconsin 13
Anderson, Judith 150
Andrew, Thomas Speer 114
Appleton, Wisconsin 90, 141
Argyle, Wisconsin 65, 66
Armstrong, Dwight 14-17
    Karleton 14-15
Army Math Research Center 14
Arreola, Philip 153
Ashland, Wisconsin 82
Ashland County 81
Ashland Daily Press 81
Asmuth, Helen 67
    James 67
Association of College Unions
    International 79
Atlanta 100
Avery, William 25

B

Bad River 81
Badger Army Ammunition Plant 14
Bald eagles 132
Balzer, Julius 162
    Mary 162
    William 162

Banach, Stan 121
Bangor, Wisconsin 34
Banks, Harmon 53
Banta, Geoffrey 79
Baraboo, Wisconsin
    15, 36, 61, 125
Barnard, Charles 111
Barney, Lawrence 11
Barre Mils 79
Bates, Cad 55-59, 150
    Tom 17
Bauman, Billy 84
Beaton, Finlay 133
Beaver Dam Argus 41
Beck, Berit 141-142
    Diane 142
Beloit, Wisconsin 63, 140, 148, 156
Beloit Daily News 106
Bembenek, Lawrencia 126-132
    Virginia 131
Bennett, Debra 83, 84
    William R. 84
Bequette, Joseph 69
Berkeley Barb 17
Beth Israel Center 152
Bethany-St. Joseph Care Center 33
Birdsall, Lucille 26
Biskupic, Vince 68
Bitney, Woodrow 39
Black Earth, Wisconsin 28
Black, Joe 140
Black Panther Party 15
Blackstone, Barbara 64-66
    Tom 65-66
Blanchardville, Wisconsin 65
Bloomington, Indiana 16
Boatwick Trailer Court 79
Bober, Karl 19
    Raymond 18
Borck, Rocky 91
Boston Store 129
Boy Scouts 21
Boyer, Edward L. 118
Briarmoon, Nathan 69
Brier, Harold 128

Bringe, Lorelei 121-122
        Mark 121-122
Brittingham Bay 117
Brookview Mobile Home Park 91
Brown, Kim 65
Brothers II 52
Buchanan, Stanley 135
Buehl, Albert 51
Buerger, Harry 29
Burlington, Wisconsin 66
Burt, Leo 14, 17
Burton, Bill 98
Byrd, Charles 124

C

Cady, Cheryl 134
Caffee, William 44, 45
Calumet County 75
Calvert, Walker 44
Cambridge, Wisconsin 159
Canada 17, 130
Capital Times 37, 38
Capitol Square 106, 107
Cardinal Hotel 84
Carter, Shameika 85
Carthage College 72
Carver, Jonathan 18
Cathedral Christ the King Church
        111
Cathedral School 111
Central High School 21
Champaign, Illinois 154
Charles, Father Fiore 36
Charleston, Illinois 19
Chicago 14, 60, 61, 67, 71, 79,
        94, 118, 140, 150,
        153, 156
Chicago Daily Times 120
China 26
Christian, Carrie 61, 62
        Catherine 101-103
        Kathy 63
        Robert 61-62
Civil Air Patrol 21

Civil War 12
Cleveland, Mississippi 85
Cocroft, Joseph 25
Coffey, William 162, 163
Cohen, Louis 136
Cole, Cory 134
Collard, Howard 108
Collins, Marvin 73
Columbia County 29, 134
Columbus, Wisconsin 108
Comstock, Wisconsin 146
Concord, Wisconsin 52, 80
Concord Recreation Center 52, 80
Contreraz, Geraldine 101
Cooke, John Peyton 10
Cosmo Club 103
Cronin-Hovland Liquor Store 51
Croteau, Joe 81
Cuba 17
Currie, Elmer 136

D

Daily Cardinal 14
Dairy Queen 52
Dane, Wisconsin 36-37
Dane County
        9, 36, 37, 84, 101, 104, 106
Darlington, Wisconsin 44
Daytona Beach, Florida 99
DDT 132
Dean Clinic 161
Dean, Joseph P. 137
Deneen, Timothy 100
Depies, Laurie 12, 13
Destrampe, Helen 42, 43
Detroit 122
Dickerson, Rasheda 160
Dieckmann, June 47
Divine Savior Hospital 30
Dodgeville, Wisconsin 84
Doe, Jane 22
Doerr, Thomas 32
Dolowy, Herbert 79
        Terry 78-79

168 • *101 Wisconsin Unsolved Mysteries*

Don Quixote Supper Club 26
Donovan, Anthony 119
Door County 143
Dosch, Grant 136
Doty Island 67
Douglas County 110
Douglass, Michael 35
Dousman, Hercules 35
Drew, Kelly 28, 52, 53, 80
Dungeons and Dragons 69
Durfee, Michael 129

E

E. Jaccard Co. 35
Eagle River, Wisconsin 152
Eau Claire, Wisconsin
    10, 11, 83, 98
Eau Claire County 32
Eberius, Linda 56
Edgerton, Wisconsin 88
Edgerton High School 88
Eischen, Cherilyn 90
Eisenberg, Donald 132
Elkhorn, Wisconsin 76, 89
Elkhorn Independent 76
Elliott, James 106
    Julie 106
Evanson, Evan 10
Evansville, Wisconsin 69

F

Farrior, Sheila 147
Fassnacht, Robert 14
FBI 36, 95, 154
Fennimore, Wisconsin 105
Finch, Wanda 159
Fine, David 14, 15, 16
Fisher, Herbert 65
    Michael 110-113
    Valerie 110
Fitchburg, Wisconsin 102
Flom, Jay Kelly 54
Florida 63
Foeste, Arthur 86

Folts, Perry 151
Fond du Lac, Wisconsin 141
Fond du Lac County Jail 130
Fort Atkinson, Wisconsin 47, 52
Fox Lake Correctional Institution 58
Fox River Mall 12
Fox Valley 67
Foye, John 119
Fredrickson, Jerry 23
Friendship, Wisconsin 73, 135
Frydenland, James 91-92
    Jessica, 6
    Mathew, 91
Fyfe, Beatrice 81

G

Gage, Michael 33
Gaik, Stanley 82
    Walter 81-82
Gallagher, Frances 45-46
Gates, T. Perry 96
Gehrt, Marilyn 129
Gein, Ed 22, 149-150
Genna, Anthony 155
    Mark 155
Germantown, Maryland 37
Ghost Riders 63, 101-102
Gibson, William 40, 41
Giuliani, August 94
Glimme, Eddie 103
Goin, Laurin 57
Gollmar, Robert 22, 150
Good 'N Loud Music 9
Grand Rapids, Wisconsin 56
Grann, James 10
Granton, Wisconsin 18
Gray, Earl 91
Green Bay, Wisconsin 26
Griffin, Maryetta 24
Griffith, Randy 61
Griswold, Dave 90
Guardian Angels 65
Gugliatto, Nick 130, 131
Gurnee, Illinois 95

H

Hack, Timothy 28, 52, 80
Hackl, Angela 65
Haese, William 130
Hall, Betty 105
    Donne 105
    Julie Ann 105-106
    Larry 12
Hales, Hattie Sherman 162
Hamblin, Gary 37
Hamm, Patricia 101, 104
Hammernik, Jean 42-43
    Jerome 43
    Jerry 42
Harmony Grove, Wisconsin 134
Harpt, Tom 93
Harris, Debra 113
    Mary 86
    Wanda 157
Hartley, Evelyn 19, 150
Haskins, David 158
Haunted Heartland 44
Hayes, Claude 74
Hebron, Wisconsin 52
Hecht, Joey 129
Hegge, Al 101, 103
Hendrickson, Virginia 158-159
    Phillip 159
Herker, Charles 40
Herrell, Vern 74
Hinshaw, Arnold 17-18
    Ginger 17-18
History of Dodge County 41
Hogan, Mary 149, 150
Holtz, Roger 42
Honor Snacks 152
Hoover, Herbert 17
Horenberger, Frederick 130
Horicon, Wisconsin 40
Horicon War 41
Hornbostel, Lloyd 63
Horne, Scott 92
Horseshoe Bay 143
Hudson, Carolyn 129

Huebner, Dale 151
    Lori 151
Huntington, Robert 123

I

Illinois 13, 142
Iola, Wisconsin 30
Iowa 56
Iowa County 84
Ironwood Hospital 81
Isle Royale 63
Israel 153
Italian Evangelical Church 94
Ixonia, Wisconsin 53

J

Jack, Ralph "Creeper" 104
Jackson, C.D. 148
Jacobs, Russell 43
Jaeger, Richard 48, 74
Janesville, Wisconsin
    51, 68, 69, 89, 106, 151, 158
Janesville Academy of Beauty
    Culture 52
Janesville Gazette 89
Jefferson, Wisconsin 88
Jefferson County
    29, 48, 52, 54, 80, 102
Jeter, Vernell 86
Johnson, John A. "Dogskin" 118, 121
    Bertha, 118
Jones, George "Mule" 25, 55, 72, 85, 105, 113, 137, 143, 154, 157, 160
    Robert 109
Joseph, Frank 64
Joyce Funeral Home 86
Juneau County 73
Justl, Mark 86

K

Kaczynski, Ted 17

Kammer, Bonnie 153
    Gregg 152-153
Kanieski, Colleen 59
    Eddie Jr 57-58
    Edward 55-59
Kaukauna, Wisconsin 12
Keeler, Leonarde 120
Kellner, Wisconsin 55
Kelly, Woody 94
Kenosha, Wisconsin
    66, 72, 94, 115
Kirkwood, Missouri 50
Kleinheinz, Bruno 117
Kliman, Irwin 39
    Sheldon 39
Kohler, Martin 129
Konicek, Paul 100
Kopp, Steve 70
Kortte, Debbie 88
Kraemer, Erik 146
Krnak, Allen 47
    Andrew 48-49
    Thomas 47
Kubler-Ross, Elizabeth 34
Kunz, Alfred 36
Kutczewski, Norbert 28, 54

L

La Crescent, Minnesota 96
La Crosse, Wisconsin
    19, 22, 33, 78, 91, 96, 150
La Crosse State University 20
La Crosse Tribune 83
Lacke, Jerome 104
Lafayette County 65
LaFleur, David Jr. 159
Lake County, Illionis 95
Lake Geneva, Wisconsin 67
Lake Geneva Playboy Club 128
Lake Mendota 87
Lake Michigan 94
Lake Mills, Wisconsin 63
Lake Monona 92
Lake Superior 63

Lake Winnebago 67
Lake Wisconsin 134
Lamont, Robert 17, 19
Land O' Lakes, Wisconsin 17
LaPorte, David 40
Lawrence, Rev. Brey 38
Laws, Dorothy 137
Lee, Peter 26
Lee, Russell 79
LeMahieu, Susan 139
Lemberger, Alois 120
    Annie 116-120
    Martin 120, 121
Lent, Richard 75
Lindholm, Dave 147
Lindstrom, Hans 76
Littel, Brian 100-102
    Gordon 101-102
Little Falls, New York 15
Little Muskego Lake 42
Lodi, Wisconsin 134
Lone Rock, Wisconsin 65
Lucas, Henry Lee 54, 106, 125, 161
Lulling, Charles 87
Luna, Ruperto 148
Luther Hospital 11
Lyndon Station, Wisconsin
    64, 65, 66
Lynn, Janna Henningsen 75

M

Maas, Stephen 160
Maasch, Lloyd 30
MacKenzie Environmental Educa-
    tion Center 29
Madison 9, 10, 14, 15, 44-45,
    49, 58, 59-60, 71, 77,
    83, 86, 92, 98-100, 102,
    105, 107, 114, 116, 124,
    129, 136, 139, 150, 152,
    154-155, 161
Madison Area Technical College
    125
Madison Diocese 38

Madison East High School 139
Madison Memorial High School 152
Main-King Tap 106
Malchow, Steve 13
Malloy, Michael 47
Manders, Michelle 27, 54
Maniece, Debra 143
Maroney, Thomas 33
Marquette University 50, 128
Marquez, Jose 148
Maurer, Chad 59-61
        Dolly 61
        John 60
Mauston, Wisconsin 73
May, Wayne 64
McCarthy, Scott 148
McCartney, Doug 103
McCaul, Richard 151
McClendon, Willie 53
McCormick, Florence 25, 104
McDonald, John Jr 142
McFadden, Susan 125, 126
McGrath, John 146
McHenry, Illinois 67
McIntyre, Marilyn 108
McKenzie, Dean 89
McManus, Jack 75
Meitner, Bria 134
Menasha, Wisconsin 12
Mendota Mental Health Institute
        119, 150
Merrill, Wisconsin 157
Merrillville, Indiana 114
Meyer, Mark R. 98
Meyers, Frank 75
Michigan 112
Middleton, Wisconsin 142
Midway Tavern 96
Miller, Dawn 68
        John 66
        Roger 31
        Russell 68-70
        Tanya 72
Mills, Mike 94
Milton, Wisconsin 88

Milwaukee, Wisconsin 15, 24,
        28, 49, 53-55, 72, 85,
        93, 104, 113, 126, 128,
        130, 137, 143-144, 147,
        152-153, 157, 160
Milwaukee County Jail 157
Milwaukee Journal-Sentinel 147
Milwaukee Police Department 129
Mims, Joyce Ann 85
Mineral Point, Wisconsin 44
Mini Stop and Shop 88
Minneapolis. Minnesota 11, 91
Minnesota 112, 125
Minocqua 112
Mirror Lake State Park 125
Mississippi River 20, 96
Molnar, Tim 99, 100
Monroe, Wisconsin 36
Montana 63
Monterrey Mills 89
Mork, Gerald 30, 32, 33
        William 31
Morrison, Clair 23
Morrison, Lila 23
Mraz, Donna 49
Munro, Victor 51
Muskego, Wisconsin 42

N

Nachreiner, Linda 65
Naughty But Nice Adult Bookstore
        140, 156
Neenah, Wisconsin 27, 67, 95
Nelson, Barbara 88
        Rebecca Ann 88
        Terry 88
New Lisbon High School 64
New Odanah, Wisconsin 81
New Richmond, Wisconsin 146
New York 63, 72
New York City 65
Nicaragua 17
Nicholas, Derek Anderson 48
Norman, Michael 44

Norman, Oklahoma 16
North Western Railroad 115
Northwestern University 120

O

Oakhill Correctional Institution 98
Ocean Beach, California 15
Oconomowoc, Wisconsin 54
Oconomowoc High School 80
Odanah, Wisconsin 81
Odom, Karen 69
O'Hare Airport 153
Ohio 66, 99
O'Leary, David 69
Olsen, George 18
Olson, Dale 42
Omernick, Ronald 157
            Vickie 157, 158
On Death and Dying 34
Ontonagon, Wisconsin 81
Ore-Ida Foods 135
Oregon 16
Oregon School of Law 16
Orlowski, Richard 110
Oscar Mayer 92
Oshkosh, Wisconsin 12, 90
Outagamie, Wisconsin 33

P

Palace Theater 39
Park Place Restaurant 86
Park Village Apartments 106
Paul, William 95
Paulson, Dean 159
Peters, Warren 54
Petersborough, Ontario 15
Peterson, James 89
Phillippines 115
Phil's Refrigeration Service 51
Picnic Point 87
Piggy's 79
Pingitore, Antonio 66
Pinkerton 67
Pipe Lake 146

Plainfield, Wisconsin 22, 149, 150
Platteville, Wisconsin 162
Playboy Club 126
Please Pass the Roses 59
Plier, Donald 123
Plover, Wisconsin 135
Polk County Sheriff's Department
    147
Portage, Wisconsin 30, 122, 123
Portage County 32
Portland Oregonian 17
Post-Kammer, Phyllis 153
Potter, John 59
Potts, Nancy 75
Poynette, Wisconsin 29, 121
Prairie Dells Park 158
Prairie du Chien, Wisconsin 35
Preston, Ophelia 55
Proctor, Ann 95
Pryzbilla, Alan 82
            Aloyzie 82-83
            Leon 82-83
"Psycho" 149

Q

Quamme, Orval 48

R

Racine, Wisconsin 97
Racine Bible Church 142
Raczkowski, Dorothy 135
Radisson La Crosse Hotel 79
Rads 17
Rahn, Carolyn 109
Rand, Paul 114
Rasmusen, Viggio 20
            Janis 20
Ray, David 27
Ray-O-Vac Inc. 87
Reardon, Antoinette 50
Red Caboose Day Care Center 125
Reichhoff, Kenny Ray 59, 73-74
Reserve Officers Training Corps
    (ROTC) 15

Reyes, Connie 115
Reynolds, Richard 28
  William 22
  Yvonne 153
Richardson, David 142
Richardson's cave 142
Ridgeway, Wisconsin 84
Riphon, Ed 107
River Falls, Wisconsin 20
River Forest High School 79
Riverside Cemetery 31
Roach, Jessica 13
Robins, Ira 129, 131
Rock County 140, 148, 151, 156
Rock Lake 63
Rock River 29
Rock Springs 101
Rockford, Illinois 148
Rosa's Cantina 63, 102
Rothschild, Christine 49, 71
Ruf, David 44
Running, Marshall 11

S

Sacred Heart Hospital 83
Sago, Walter 148
Sanchez, Hector Reuben 54
San Francisco, California 15
San Rafael, California 15
Sauk City, Wisconsin 65, 162, 163
Sauk County 48, 62, 126
Schenk's Corners 136
Schertz, Beverly 32
  Michael 31-33
Schilling, Ervin 73
Schmidt, Donald 53
Schreiner, Dan 83
Schubert, Officer 97
Schultz, Christine 126-127, 130, 132
  Elfred 126, 128-129
  Sean 128
Scott, Beth 44
Scullion, Donald 101
Senn High School 71

Shanks, Alan 62
Sheppard, Ed 141
Sjoberg, Catherine 29, 54, 80
Skierawski, Michael 130
Slater, JoAnn 115
Smith, Linford 86
Soglin, Paul 77
  Rose 78
  Sara 78
Sorenson, May 120, 121
Spanbauer, David 12
Speerschneider, Julie 124-125
Spiritland Cemetery 150
Spooner, Wisconsin 39
St. John, Hillary 134
St. Louis, Missouri 35, 154
St. Mary's Hospital 137
St. Michael's Catholic Church 36
Stanford, Terryl 140
State Crime Lab 74, 82, 112, 122
State Department of Natural
  Resources 92
State Division of Criminal Investiga-
  tion 75
Steinbicer, Mrs. Frank 76
Steinhorst, Virgil 126
Sterling Hall 14, 71, 72
Stevens Point, Wisconsin 32
Stewart, Shirley 161
Stock, Edward G. 110
Stolen, Ole A. 120
Stoughton, Wisconsin
  63, 101, 102, 124
Strangstalien Valley 23
Sturtevant, Wisconsin 141
Summerwind 17
Sun Prairie, Wisconsin 98, 122
Sun Prairie News 98
Sundby, Elmer 10
Superior, Wisconsin 110, 112, 133
Superior Evening Telegram 110
Superior Jaycees 111
Superior Telegram 133

T

Talidis, Betty 122
Taycheedah state prison 130
Templin, Albert 94
Texas 106
Texas Rangers 35
The Carver Effect 19
The Tangled Web 59
"The Texas Chainsaw Massacre."
 149
The Zoo 159
Thunder Bay, Ontario 130
Tim Hack Agricultural Award 54
Tony's Chop Suey Restaurant 125
Toole, Ottis 106, 125, 161
Toronto, Ontario 15
Torsos 10
Trempealeau, Wisconsin 82
Trempealeau County 82
Trinity St. Luke's Lutheran School
 27
Turtle Creek Campground 156
Turtle Lake High School 146

U

U.S. Army 67
Unabomber 17
Union, Illinois 122
University Hospital 58
University of Wisconsin Arboretum
 140
University of Wisconsin-LaCrosse
 78
University of Wisconsin-Madison
 9, 14, 16, 71-72, 105, 152
"Unsolved Mysteries" 100
UW-Madison Law School 87

V

Valdez, Miguel Rivera 148
Van Brunt & Davis Co. 41
Van Veghel, Jack 26
Vancouver, British Columbia 16

Vendela, Richard 110
Vernon County 22, 79
Verona, Wisconsin 142
Vietnam War 14, 98
Vilas County 17
Villa Louis State Historical Site 35
Village Pedaler 60
Viroqua, Wisconsin 22
Vollbrecht, Terry 65

W

Wabash, Indiana 12, 142
Wagner, Ruth 98
Wagner-Richardson, Derby 97-98
Walker House 44
Walworth County 89
Watertown, Wisconsin 27-28, 54
Waukegan, Illinois 54
Waukesha, Wisconsin 99
Waukesha County 100
Waukesha Freeman 43
Waunakee, Wisconsin
 100, 103, 105
Waupaca, Wisconsin 41
Waupaca County 31, 33
Waupun, Wisconsin 141
Waupun State Prison 58, 119, 163
Wausau, Wisconsin 157
Weathermen 14
Weber, Eddie 26
Weckler, Georgia Jean 150
Wegner, Glenn 34
 Linda 33, 34
 Mary 13
Wellner, Korinne 42, 43
Wells, Monsignor Thomas 37
West Bay Lake 17
Westby, Wisconsin 22
Westport, town of 161
Widness, Martin 133
Weibel, Celia 91
 Leroy 91
Wilkie, Horace 58

William Burns Detective Agency
    118
Williams, Daniel 31
         Edwin 75
         Hazel 45
Willows Tavern 103
Wilson, Annette 129
Winnebago County 68, 90
Winnefeld, Julius 40
Wipperfurth, David 37
Wisconsin Crime Lab (see State
    Crime Lab)
Wisconsin Dells 65, 125, 135
Wisconsin Historical Society 105
Wisconsin Rapids, Wisconsin
    55, 56, 150
Wisconsin State Journal 9, 13, 24,
         28-29, 47, 48, 51, 62-64,
         74, 93, 98, 118, 123,
         153-154, 156
Wisconsin Supreme Court 58
Wisconsin Tissue Mills 68
Wisconsin-Minnesota Light and
    Power Company 10
Wisconsin's innocent convict
    compensation law 75
Wissler, Jacob 129
Woeherer, Mary 130
Wood County 59
Woodland Investment Co 95
Worden, Bernice 149, 150
World War I 76, 94
Wosepka, Ray 9

Y

Yahara River 124
Younger, George 117

Z

Zaleski, Rob 38
Zapata, Eugene 154
         Jeanette 154
Zess, Judy 127, 128
Zion, Illinois 54, 94